go!games

OPTICAL ILLUSIONS

By Gianni A. Sarcone

imagine!
Publishing

10 9 8 7 6 5 4 3 2

An Imagine Book
Published by Charlesbridge
85 Main Street
Watertown, MA 02472
617-926-0329
www.imaginebooks.net

Printed in China

ISBN 978-1-62354-022-7

TABLE OF CONTENTS

INTRODUCTION

A Zen monk once dreamed that he was a fluttering butterfly. During the course of the dream, he lost his individuality as a person and became the insect. Waking with a start, he was utterly disoriented and had to ask himself, "Am I a man who dreams about being a butterfly, or am I a butterfly who dreams about being a man?"

Just as the dream distorted the monk's notion of what is true, the optical illusions in this book have been designed to perplex you and challenge you to question the nature of reality.

What you perceive depends mainly on your brain, which interprets visual information received as electrical signals from the eyes. However, by applying knowledge of how things should look, the brain can often misinterpret the data and cause us to misperceive images, even when we know that what we are seeing cannot be correct.

These two incredible jelly balls beneath your forehead are able to capture all the animated and material things that surround you. As soon as you open your eyes, the whole world pops into them.

The only limit of the eyes is the visual horizon. Therefore, sight gives more information about your surroundings than any of the other four senses. Unlike the other sense organs, the eye can be controlled in that if you don't want to see something, you can simply close your eyelids. (Alas, there are no ear, nose, or skin lids!)

What is an optical illusion?
Sometimes, the brain deceives the eyes. This is when differences occur between your perception or expectation of what you are seeing and the image actually received by your eyes. For example, when you perceive something that is not present, or when you incorrectly perceive what is present, then you are experiencing an optical illusion. For centuries, scientists have been studying optical illusions to help us understand how the brain works. However, most of these illusions are still not properly understood.

Illusions are often used as educational or improvement tools. In fact, stepping outside your comfort zone and thinking in ways that are both creative and challenging to your visual perception is a kind of exercise that may increase your brain flexibility. Just as going to the gym keeps you physically fit, completing visual puzzles will keep you mentally fit.

You will discover in this book that even the simplest geometrical optical illusion can produce strong visual effects, and that some optical illusions are very difficult to overcome; they remain compelling even when you are fully aware that what you see is incorrect. Ranging from simple scintillation effects to impossible staircases and concealed creatures, this book includes a selection of amazing visual illusions that are designed to stretch the limits of your perception and enable you to experience the impossible and marvel at the miraculous.

G.Sarcone

Author, artist, and researcher in the field of visual perception

PART 1:
Puzzles with No Explanation

Cylindrical Anamorphosis

Anamorphosis is a kind of art that distorts an object so that it is only revealed from a single vantage point or from its reflection on a mirrored surface. This artistic process, which involves geometry, was first attempted during the Renaissance and became exceedingly popular during the Victorian era. In the picture you can see two kinds of cylindrical anamorphosis. The upper picture shows an interesting circular pattern that turns into a set of cubes. The lower picture is from OOZ & OZ Morph-O-Scopes, Sports of All Sorts kit. The company has produced mirror anamorphosis art, toy kits, and activities for children since 1993.

Op'art Illusion
Wow! The central blurred strokes
seem to move and throb.

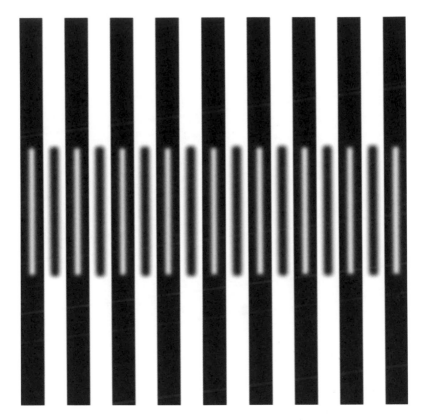

Magic Rope

The rope seems to thread through nine short deformed
tubes set in a circle. Strangely enough, the open
ends of each tube don't match up!

Impossible Urban Furniture
The main reason dogs do not like impossible structures.

Tessellated Judokas
Escher-esque interlaced martial artists! The judokas dressed in white throw their opponents dressed in black (and vice versa) symbolizing the concept of yin-yang, which describes how polar opposites or seemingly contrary forces are interconnected and interdependent in the natural world. This picture was taken from the book *Parcelles d'Infini* by French artist Alain Nicolas (Edition pour la Science).

Universal Child
You will notice that this picture of a child's face is itself composed of photographs of children. This is what artists call a composite figure. Look at the image from a distance to appreciate it best.

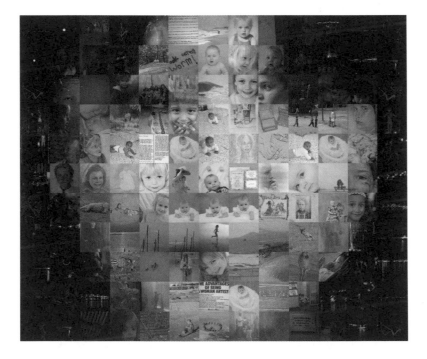

Experiment: Spotting the Blind Spot

There are no photoreceptors where the optical nerve "enters" our eye. This region where we cannot see is commonly referred to as our blind spot. You can experience your own by doing the following:

Close your right eye and hold this picture about ten to twelve inches (25–30 cm) from your left eye. Look at the dot between the magician's eyes and slowly move the page forward and back until one heart on the playing card disappears. This will happen when light rays reflected from the heart symbol fall on your blind spot.

Just Tools
Figure out the twenty-eight tools hidden in the picture!

Young Girl with Cat

No, your eyes aren't going funny. The cat really has four eyes! What is interesting about double-eyed illusions is that people have trouble seeing them. What makes your eyes dizzy is the fact they are trying to focus while your brain is fighting to give you the most coherent image of a cat.

Moving Bands

If you concentrate on the circular gray bands, you may see a vibrating fluid moving around, and without thinking about it, you may soon enter a deep, peaceful, hypnotic trance. This illusion is ideal for hypnotizers! This is called a lateral inhibition phenomenon.

Bold the A

To enlarge one of the letters "a," do as follows: stare at the cross in diagram B for about twenty to thirty seconds; then, look at the cross in diagram A. You should see the letter on your right becoming larger and bolder! (The experiment works better under a bright light.) This is an original aftereffect experiment.

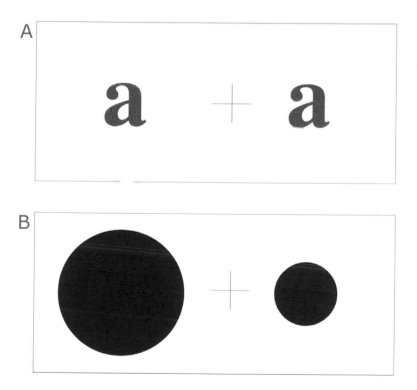

A

B

Illusive Pencils

Hold a blue pencil and a red pencil level in front of you.
Focus on them. Slowly bring the tips of the two pencils
together. No problems? Try the same thing with just one
eye open. Easy or not so much? Each eye sees from a
slightly different angle (*binocular disparity*). Both eyes
work together to give us depth perception, which you
need for your brain to be able to judge distance. When
you only use one eye, you lose depth perception.
Depth perception is also dependent on colors; objects
with warm colors tend to be seen as nearer than objects
with cold colors.

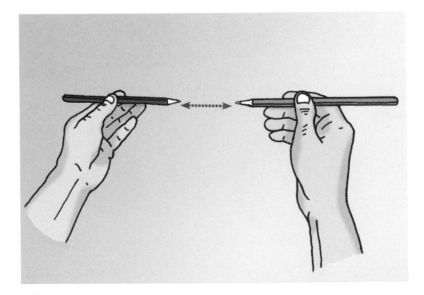

Every Way Takes You Up!

You can go up in two opposite directions on these magic stairs.

Summer Absurdities

Just enjoy this ambiguous picture that contains three absurdities. Hint: follow the shoreline.

It's Your Imagination

We bet many of you wish this pretty girl were really there. Sorry, it's just your imagination. In fact, your brain fills in the missing contours to get a coherent image.

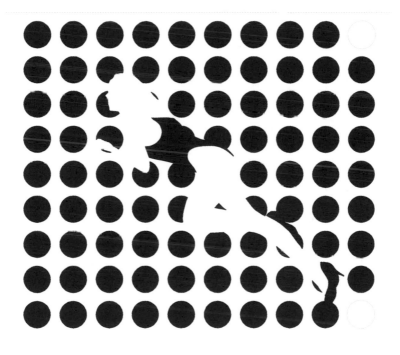

Labor vs. Capital
This is an interesting old satirical optical illusion. Actually, it is easy to spot the differences when you look closely at the picture. The two images seem, however, almost the same when viewed from a distance.

THE DIFFERENCE BETWEEN LABOR AND CAPITAL.

Dominant Vision

Just as the majority of us are either right- or left-handed, we also have a dominant eye that processes information fifteen to twenty milliseconds faster than the other. The brain uses this dominant image as the main frame of reference.

Discover which is your dominant eye is by rolling up a sheet of plain white paper. While keeping both eyes open, look down the tube and focus on your hand. Now, close your left eye and hold the tube up to your right eye (figure A). If the position of your hand is unchanged, you are right-eye dominant. If your hand jumps out of sight, you are left-eye dominant. To check your findings, open both eyes and refocus on your hand through the tube again, holding it to your left eye and closing your right eye (figure B). The results will be exactly reversed.

Uphill Motion Illusion

A gravity hill, also known as a magnetic hill (and some-times a mystery hill), is a place or a road where the layout of the surrounding land produces the optical illusion that a very slight downhill slope appears to be an uphill one. These pictures show two different views of a sloping road to Montagnaga, a small town in Italy. In the top picture, the road on the right is misperceived as running uphill. So, if you stopped your car at the Stop sign (where the three-wheeled vehicle sits in the bottom picture) and left it out of gear, it would roll backward—seemingly uphill! There are hundreds of gravity hill locations and roads around the world.

Front view

Side view

Spiraling Roman Floor Mosaic

This is a reconstitution of the oldest apparent moving pattern. In effect, when you observe the radiating pattern of tiered plumes, your eye may be fooled for a moment into thinking it is rotating slightly. We can say therefore that the first attempt to create relative movement with static images was done by Roman craftsmen. This mosaic has in its center the head of the Medusa.

Ambiguous Animals

This 2,500-year-old coin from the island of Lesbos shows perhaps one of the first ambiguous images knowingly created by man. You can see the profiles of two animals facing each other—apparently herbivores such as calves or goats—which form a third animal, a ferocious animal (maybe a wolf?) seen from the front.

Everything Moves!

There is a branch of modern art named Op'Art (short for optic art) that is concerned with visual motion, and uses optical contrasts (such as clear/dark, vertical/horizontal) to induce the illusion of motion in static images, as illustrated in this picture.

Amazing Impossible Structure

Try to mentally guess which part is perspectively incorrect in the structure. Answer: The Y-shaped structures cannot be joined together to form square patterns, unless to intentionally violate the laws of perspective.

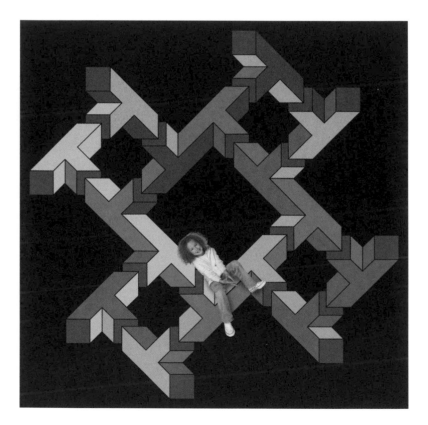

Moiré Experiments

When a repeated pattern printed on a transparent acetate sheet is laid over a second one (background pattern), the combination of both patterns creates a visual interference called moiré. Moirés are also an interesting topic to study and play with! You can make a transparent copy of the concentric texture (figure A) and combine it with its original background to create fascinating moiré effects: by translation (figures B and C), spatial translation (figure D), or compression (figure E). Moiré can also be used to create illusory movements.

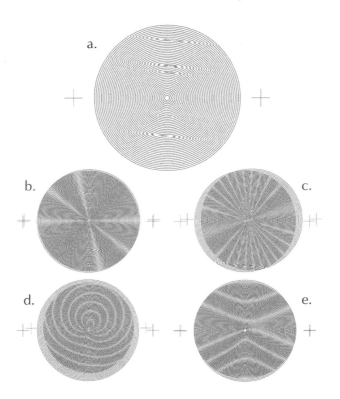

Upside-Down Town
Night follows day when the picture
is turned upside down!

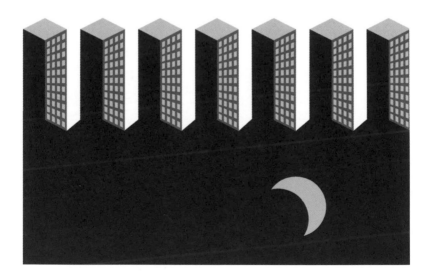

Naughty, Naughty Boys

Our grandfathers were great teases just like we are, and appreciated subtle naughty allusions and jokes! This drawing, from a German postcard (approx. 1900), plays on the ambiguity of the bald-headed gentlemen also appearing to be a lady's generous chest. Postcards with optical illusions such as this were quite popular in the early part of the last century.

Yin-Yang of Love

Here is an interesting drawing showing a figure-ground perceptual reversal, which involves alternating black-and-white elements.

Recursive Watch

The Droste effect is a kind of recursive picture that depicts an infinite reduced version of itself in a place where a similar picture would realistically be expected to appear. It can be compared to the visual experience of standing between two mirrors, seeing an infinite reproduction of one's image. To make the recursive watch shown in the picture, the photograph was cut into two distinct parts and then distorted to fit repeatedly into a logarithmic spiral, continuing this operation as long as the resolution of the picture allows.

··

PART 2:
Try These Illusions and Check Your Answers Below

··

Line A = Line B?

Line B seems longer, but are you sure?

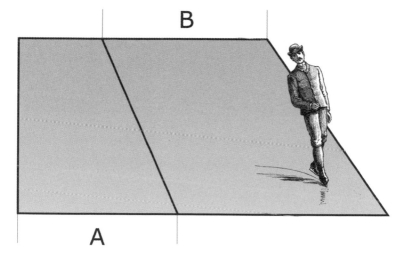

B

A

A = B ?

Three Graces?

You can see two women, but where is the lady of the night?

Answer: Standing between the two facing ladies, you can make out a third woman wearing a black dress.

Teach/Learn Dilemma

Read the word. Now, try to read it from six to ten feet (two to three meters away). What does it spell?

Magic Glass

Find a way to completely remove the
glass from the plate!

Answer: Turn the image upside down and the wine glass
will be standing outside the dish, but the name on the
card—Camilla—is still readable!

Pencil Distortion

Is the ring, formed with sliced parts of pencils, a perfect circle?

Answer: Though the inner and outer borders of the central ring seem off-center and distorted, they are concentric circles.

Come In

These bilingual notes pinned to the door indicate that the shop is open. When the shop is closed, one can use the same notes. How?

Magic Top
Move the picture from side to side to
make the top spin.

Answer: Illusory motion is induced by the visual
contrasts of the top and its background.

The Unsizable Square

Which diamond is exactly the same size as the square?

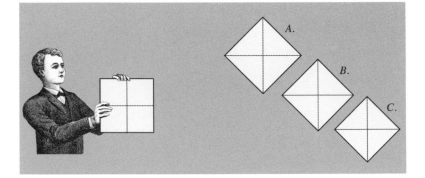

Answer: Most think it's diamond B, but the correct
answer is actually diamond A!

Curious Objects

Look at these strange items carefully. Could any of them actually exist, or are they all impossible objects?

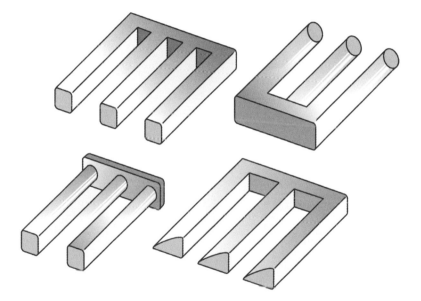

Gray Gradations
Which alignment contains squares?

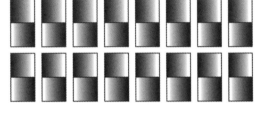

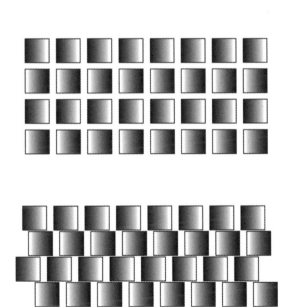

Color gradations can affect the contour and the alignment
of regular shapes. In the picture, all are squares, and
the square alignments are parallel to each other.

Ikea Tribar

Try to build this tribar by following the visual instructions. (Take a close look at the screws and the washers).

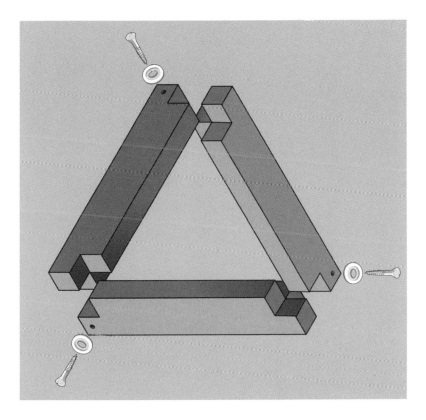

You cannot build such furniture because it is an impossible object.

Ghost Shape

Is there a square?

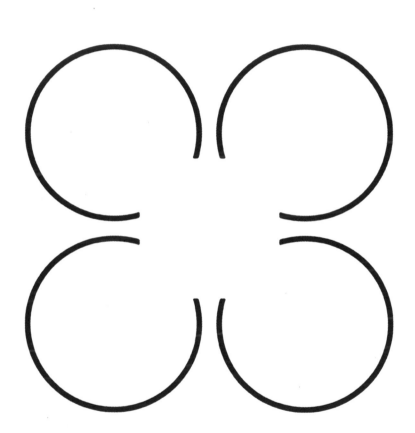

Answer: Although there is no actual printed square,
the circles end abruptly at what we perceive as the
corners of a square.

Levitation
Does the ball move slightly and levitate?

Floating Cigarette?

Is the cigarette placed between two fins or does it just float in front of the transparent structure?

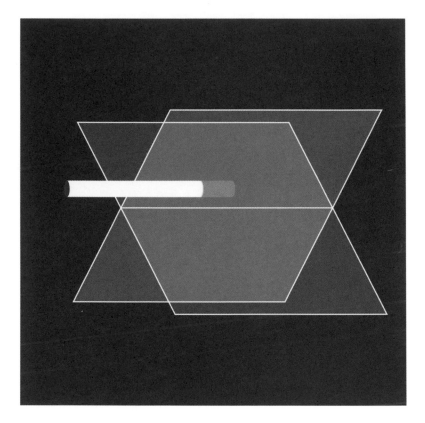

Answer: Due to contrary cues to depth perception, we cannot say which edge of these two interlocked planes is closest to us.

Sexy Droodle
What does this square of folded paper represent?

Answer: Some people see a décolleté of a beautiful woman.

In Perspective
What is wrong with this circular structure?

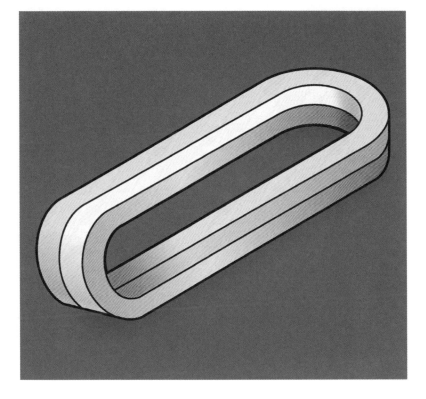

Answer: Although the straight arms of the structure
are perfectly aligned, the circular ends, in
defiance of every law of perspective, are
perpendicular to each other.

Tilting Effect

Are the vertical and horizontal sets of gray
lines straight and perpendicular to each other?

Answer: Though they appear to tilt, the vertical
and horizontal sets of gray lines are straight and
perpendicular to each other.

Bulging or Parallel?
Are the black lines bulging outward?

Answer: No, they are straight and parallel to each other. This distortion illusion is induced by the cross in the background.

Line A = Line B?
Are lines A and B the same length?

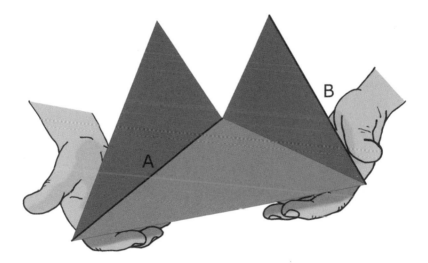

Impossible Stairs
How many steps are in this staircase?

Answer: Impossible to say, because it is
an impossible object.

Ambigrams
Turn the page over: what do you notice?

Answer: The words "sublime" and "apache" read exactly the same! Baffling, isn't it?

Scholars

Which one of the three men depicted in the illustration is the tallest?

Answer: Curiously enough, the man in the foreground is approximately 15 percent taller than the man in the background!

That's Impossible

This complex structure cannot exist in the
three-dimensional world. Why not?

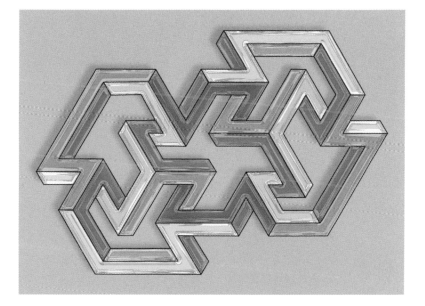

Answer: Look at how the joints meet and then
branch out. No real figure can have sides that meet
and expand in such a way.

Illusive Top Hat

In this Belle Époque picture, after a drawing by the French artist Edgar Degas, you can see a proud gentleman wearing a particular top hat. Is this top hat wider (AB) than it is tall, or taller (CD) than it is wide?

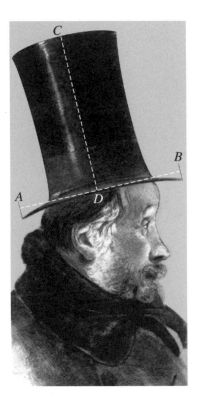

Answer: Even though it seems unbelievable, the brim of the top hat is broader than its crown!

Sailor Thoughts

On dry land, sailors typically have just one obsession.
Can you guess what the sailor is looking for?

Answer: Turn the picture upside down and
you will discover the face of a lady.

Quadrilaterals
Which geometric shape is most like the four-sided figure ABCD?

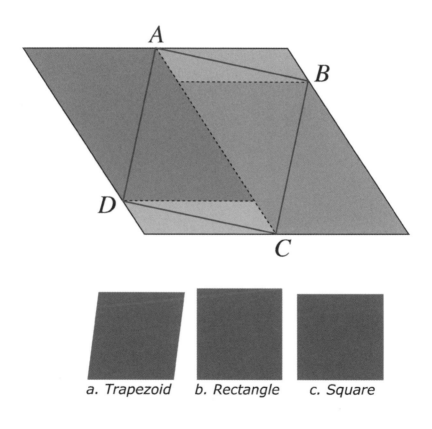

a. Trapezoid   b. Rectangle   c. Square

Answer: Most people answer B, instead of the correct solution, C.

Beware of Illusion!
What's wrong with this picture? Humor and optical illusions can be meshed together to create very odd situations.

Answer: Unfortunately for our passerby, the steps gradually turn into holes in the pavement.

Fraser Diamonds
Are the three floating concentric shapes skewed diamonds or squares? Does the background vibrate?

Answer: The three shapes that appear like slanted diamonds are in fact squares. This tilting effect is based on the Fraser spiral illusion.

Find the Figure and the Ground

The words "figure" and "ground" are both
written here. Can you find them?

Answer: Look inside "ground" to
find "figure."

A Cat Hiding

Can you tell which is the cat and which is the shadow?

Answer: The shadow is cast to the right side of the upside-down cat.

Tvins
Is the upside-down "V" darker than the right-side-up "V"?

Answer: The two "Vs" are identical, although the one on the black background appears much brighter.

Gray Discs
Can you say which spot is darker and
which one is lighter?

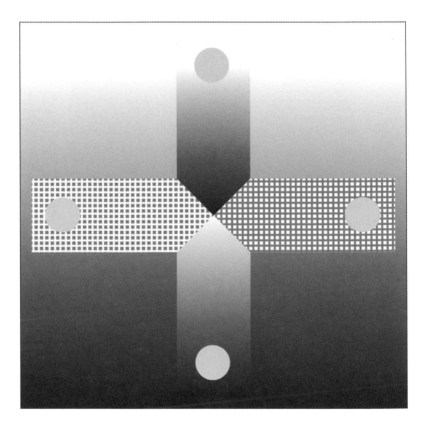

Answer: All four spots have the same brightness
and hue. The illusion is due to the simultaneous
brightness contrast effect.

Mountain Magic
Look carefully at this landscape and you
may uncover a mystery.

Answer: Do you see the sleeping face
embedded in the mountain?

Distorted by Letters

As you can see, alternating black-and-white capital letters have been distributed on a checkered surface. Are the dark and clear squares distorted?

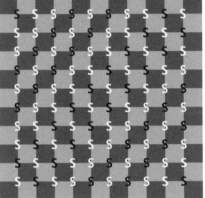

Answer: Although the upper checkered surface appears to wave and the lower one seems to shrink toward its center, all the squares are straight and aligned.

Experimental Trumpeter
What happens when the trumpeter blows the trumpet?

Answer: Nothing, because it is an
impossible trumpet.

Barking Dog

What is the dog barking at?

Answer: A cat, of course. Turn the
picture upside down.

Homage to Escher

This image contains multiple tessellating portraits of the Dutch artist M.C. Escher. What do you notice when you turn the picture upside down?

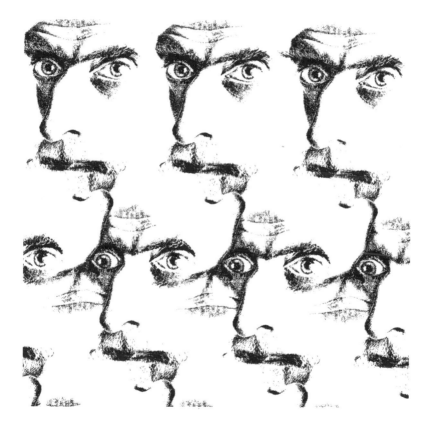

Answer: The picture is reversible. In fact, the multiple portraits can be seen both right-side up and upside down.

Very Bizarre Dogs

How many dogs can you count: one, two, three, or more?

Answer: Don't count them.
This is just an impossible figure!

Running Waters

Do the vertical gray lines twist up and down like a water flow? (Please, turn off the faucets once you have experienced the illusion!)

of our visual system.
The illusion is due to lateral inhibition
Answer: The image is static, of course.

73

Kite Pattern

Can you guess which line of bright and dark squares is most like the decorative pattern in the middle of the kite: A, B, or C?

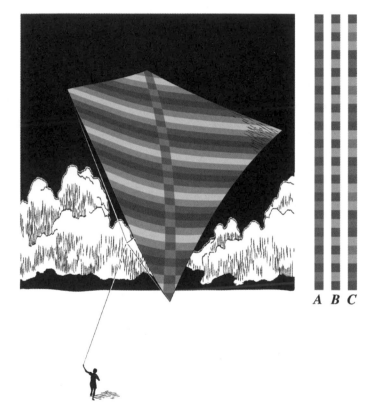

A B C

Answer: Line A. The effect that induced you to choose C instead of A is called the simultaneous brightness contrast effect.

Goliath vs. David

In figure A, Goliath appears to be taller than David, while in figure B, it looks like David is taller! Are the two sets of puzzles the same?

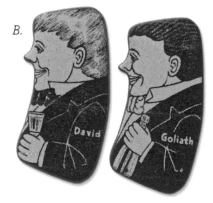

Answer: In fact, *all* the figures shown in the picture are identical in size. These kinds of "curvature effects" are called Wundt-Jastrow illusions.

Polyvalent Bookshelf
What is wrong with this bookshelf?

Good Vibes

Answer: The images do not move at all.
It is the visual disturbance due to the repetition
of bright and dark decorative elements that
causes these virtual rotations.

Special Dice
What do these dice have that is special?

Answer: These are unreal four-dimensional and eight-sided dice. Actually, the eight sides are numbered by dots from zero to seven, so placed that the sum of the dots on opposite sides equals seven.

Illusive Jet Propeller

Here is an example of autokinetic illusion. Look at the blades of these two jet propellers; now, what happens if you concentrate your gaze on the cross?

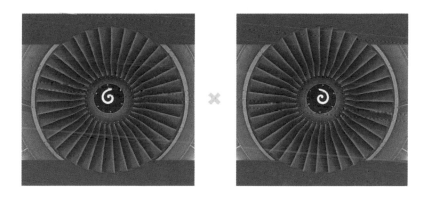

The blades of the propellers seem to rotate. The linear grayscale shade on the blades is responsible for this curious illusion known as peripheral drift illusion (PDI).

Telling Spikes

Someone is hidden within the alignment of black spikes. Can you guess who?

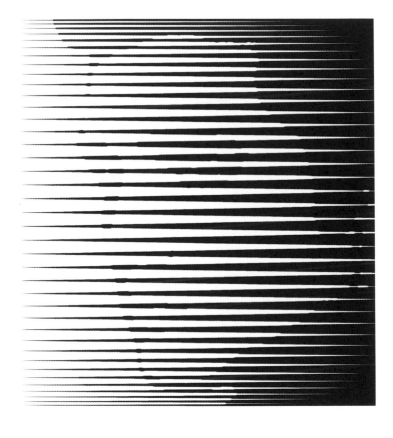

Answer: Elvis Presley—look at the picture from a distance.

Visual Oddity?
Can you see what is odd in this picture?

Answer: This is an impossible assemblage of three impossible dice.

81

Black Patches

Is this series of black patches blurred? What happens when you sweep your gaze around this pattern?

Answer: No, the black patches are solid geometric shapes and aren't blurred at all! If you sweep your gaze around the picture you may see the patches move or perceive hues of colors on the background.

Impossible Vault

Push or pull? Your money would not be safe in this incongruous vault!

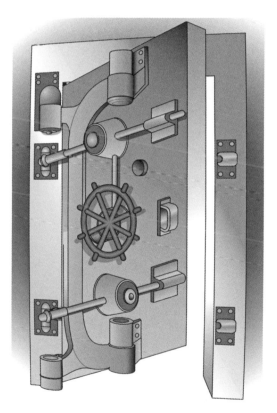

Answer: In this impossible illusion, the lower part of the reinforced door is opening away from you, while the upper side is opening toward you.

Tilting Squares
Are the squares really tilting to the left?

Answer: No, they are all perfect upright squares.
The illusion is induced by the alternating orders
of dots in the background.

Peculiar Cubic Network
Is this cubic network consistent?

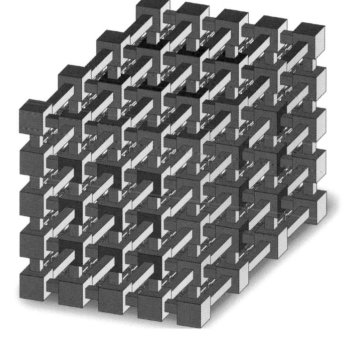

The Lonely Rower
Is the rower being watched?

Answer: Yes, if you look more carefully, you may discover the face of a smiling young woman hidden under the bridge!

Concave vs. Convex

Can you say which colander is showing its convex side, and which its concave side?

Answer: Depending on your point of view, that is, the way you perceive the direction from which the light falls, the same object may appear concave or convex.

Curious Pendulum
What's wrong with this strange device?

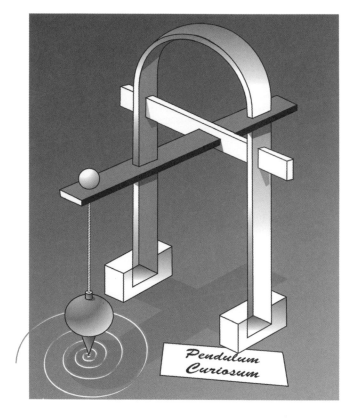

Answer: It is just an incredible invention of a mad scientist. The feet of the object cannot exist in our 3-D world, and likewise, neither can the crossings of the boards.

Bent Slats
How many slats can you count on this page?

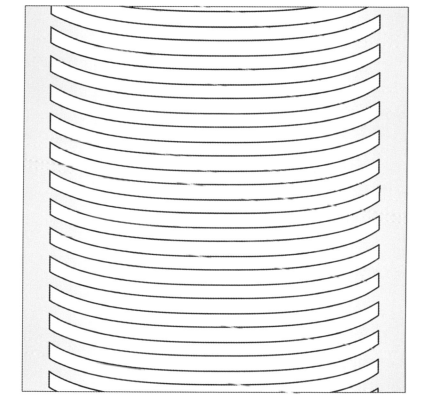

Answer: Usually, at first sight, this seems
like a bunch of oddly shaped parallelograms;
however, it is actually just one continuous line!

Evolution

Can you transform this marine mammal into a feathered animal?

Answer: With a simple turn of the page, the seal transforms into a toucan!

The Lonely Dancers
These dancers are having fun.
But are they really lonely?

Answer: A woman's face can be perceived at
the center of the illustration. This is an ambiguous
figure-ground illusion.

Ball Matching
Which ball corresponds exactly to
ball A ball B or ball C?

Answer: The answer is ball C, even if it
seems darker than ball A. This is a
simultaneous brightness contrast effect.

Puzzling Horse
Find the kissing cowgirl's boyfriend!

Answer: Have a look at the large white spot on the horse's head and you will find the silhouette of her boyfriend.

Priming Illusion

Add the numbers shown on this page in your head by following the instructions. Write down the final result on a piece of paper. Then, check the result with a calculator. Do you notice something strange?

Take 1000 and add 40 to it.

Now add another 1000.

Now add 30.

Add another 1000.

Now add 20.

Now add another 1000.

Finally, add 10.

What is the total?

What Is It?

What does this intriguing vintage picture show? A very ugly man or something completely different?

Answer: If you rotate the picture ninety-degrees clockwise, you will see a nice little puppy taking a nap!

Scattering Fluids
What occurs if you concentrate on the concentric rings?

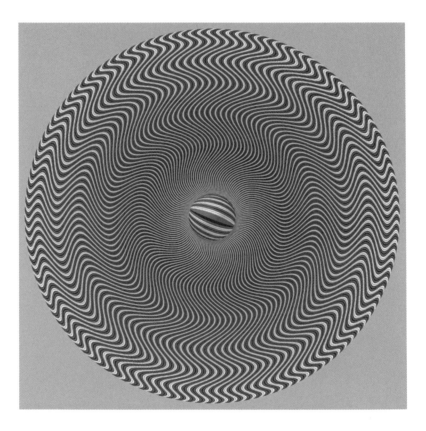

Untraceable Elephants
Find four elephants in the puzzle pieces!

Answer: The elephants are in A2, H3, F6, and D9.

Misleading Gray Stripes

Is the rectangle A wider and brighter than rectangle B?

Answer: Both rectangles are exactly the same brightness and width.

Tunnel effect

What is there to worry about in this mysterious tunnel?

Answer: So weird how the image is static but your eyes can't make the bottom of the tunnel stop expanding forward to you! Brr...

Inception

What happens if the girl climbs the
stairs up to the platform?

Answer: The platform and stairs form an
impossible continuous loop. The girl could actually
walk and climb the stairs forever and never get
any higher.

Topsy-Turvy
Where is the Scotsman?

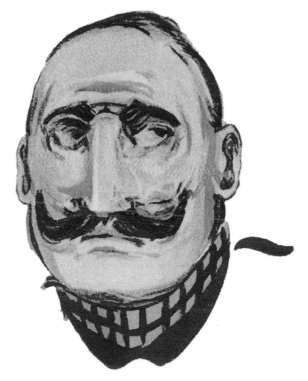

Answer: Turn the page upside down.
This is a caricature by Lord Kitchener.

Evanescence

Concentrate on the middle of the black eye for at least twenty seconds. Do you notice something strange?

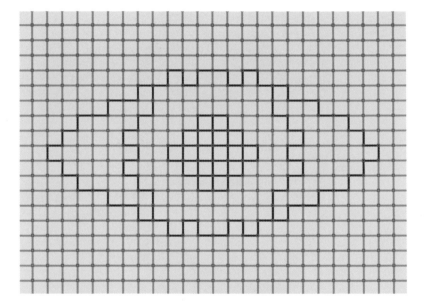

Answer: You might get the eye to completely disappear!

Ant Reckoning

Without counting them, are there more black ants or white ants? Is the square formation straight or slanted?

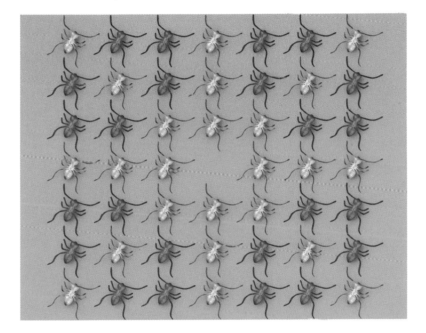

Droodle

Can you guess what this picture is? There is no right or wrong answer and your guess might even be funnier than our suggestion.

Answer: The picture represents an elephant standing on its front legs.

Hidden Giraffe

Spot the other giraffe in this exotic old engraved landscape.

Answer: Look at his neck.

Line A = Line B?
Are lines A and B the same length?

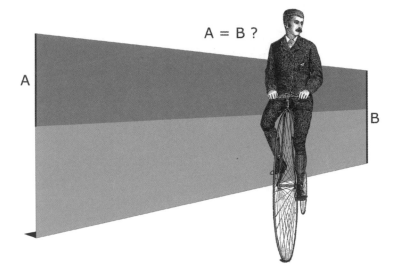

A = B ?

A

B

Answer: Yes, despite the fact they look different.
This is a variant of the Ponzo illusion.

Question of Size
Which goldfish is longer?

Answer: Both are the same size. The bottom fish seems longer because of its proximity to the glass's edge, making it appear tighter, and thus wider.

Ever-Changing Dice
How much does this dice roll add up to?
Eight? Are you sure?

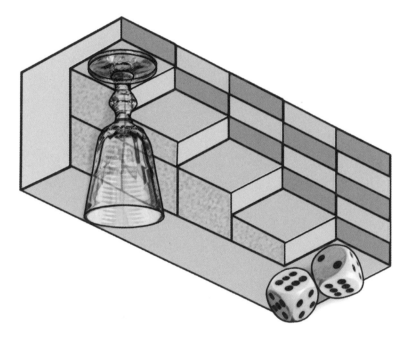

Answer: This picture can be viewed upside down just as well! If you invert the picture, the dice equal ten.

Beauty Mirage
Can you guess what this is?

Answer: The picture is only composed of
superimposed black, gray, and white dots, but if you
look at it from a certain distance, the lovely face of
Marilyn Monroe will appear!

Strange Sun Rays
Stare at the center of this radial pattern.
Do you notice something interesting?

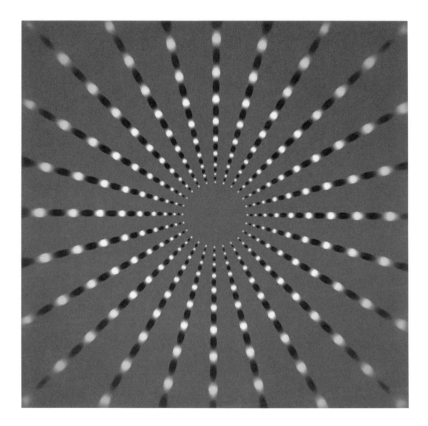

Answer: The alignments of white discs
seem to pulse like runway lights at an airport.

Happy vs. Unhappy
Which face is larger?

Answer: The smiling face seems larger, but they are actually both the same size. This illusion is known as the Ebbinghaus illusion.

A Total Diva
Someone is hidden in the sunset. Can you guess who?

Answer: It's Marilyn Monroe again!
(View the picture from a distance.)

Roman Columns

Do the columns of this Roman temple
converge or diverge?

Answer: No, they're perfectly parallel. This
interesting version of the Popple illusion shows
how vertical bars with an alignment of adequately
shifted patterns can induce a tilt sensation.

Ambiguous Cubes

Are the cubic spaces outward or inward? Are you sure?
Turn the page upside down!

Answer: The cubic spaces are ambiguous
figures and can be seen both as convex or
concave shapes.

It Moves!

What happens if you blink repeatedly
while staring at this pattern?

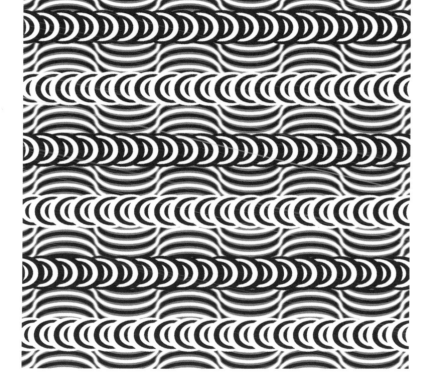

Answer: The horizontal patterned bands
seem to move to and fro.

Fix It!

Can you repair this plate? Hint: Try to concentrate on one of the lobster's eyes.

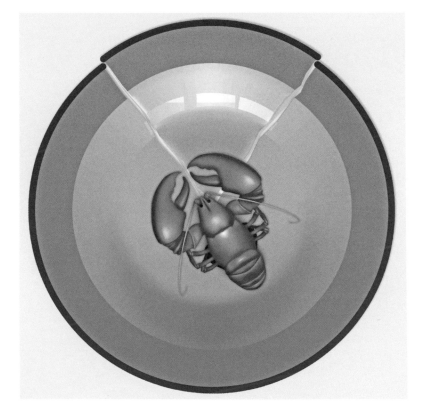

Answer: If you concentrate, after some time it will seem that the broken piece of the plate rejoins the rest. At least the outer black rim should appear unbroken.

Question of Font
Which character is wider: the W or the H?

Answer: Though the H seems wider, both are of the same width.

Checkered Flag

Are the squares A and B of the checkered flag of the same shade?

Answer: Yes, they have exactly the same color and shade! Unbelievable, isn't it? This illusion is related to the simultaneous brightness contrast effect.

Camouflage

A tourist took this photograph of a tiger while traveling in India and noticed afterward that there was a child camouflaged in the picture. Where is he?

Answer: The camouflaged profile of the child is on the tiger's cheek. (His profile is facing sideways next to the tiger's eye.)

Contact

Can you magically make the forefingers of
this fresco touch each other?

Answer: Slowly draw the image closer
to your nose, and the fingers will, at a certain
point, touch each other.

Mysterious Path
Is the line AB as long as the line AC?

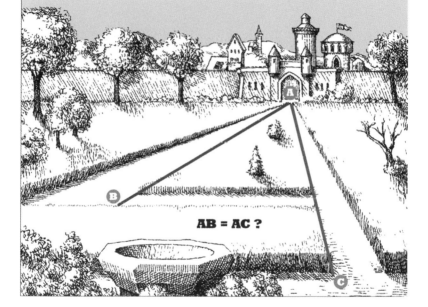

AB = AC ?

Answer: No, although 80 percent of readers
think both lines are equal. Actually the line
AB is much longer!

Divine Appearance

Find the face of Buddha in the leaves. Don't stress. Some people have taken up to fifteen minutes to find it!

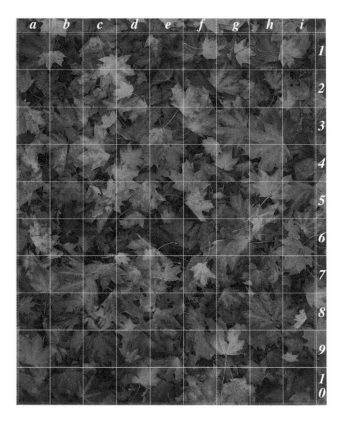

Answer: The face of Buddha is in C8.

Perceptual Set

Though the picture is mostly dark and incomplete,
thanks to our prior perception experiences we can see a . . .

Answer: . . . man bowing and taking his hat
off. Perceptual set is a predisposition to
perceive something in relation to prior
perceptual experiences.

Aloha!

There are two important errors hidden in this image.
Your mission is to spot them both!

Answer: 1. She has two right feet; 2. she has six
fingers on her left hand (counting the
concealed thumb).

Pretender

My fishmonger swore by outstretching his arms, "The fish I caught was this big!" Then I told him that his fabulous fish was taller than him! Am I right or wrong?

Answer: If you measure the distance between the arms from the left to the right hand, the fish is actually longer than the height of the fishmonger.

Self-Made Bicycle
Will the front wheel of this bicycle turn freely?

Answer: No. It cannot roll because it is an impossible object. If you observe the front "wheel," carefully, you will notice that it is both a flat hexagon and a solid cube.

Radial Discs

Do you notice something unusual in these sun-like shapes?

Answer: Although they are static, the central discs appear to scintillate and rotate.

Rectangle Differences

Is the top rectangle (A) the same as the second one (B) in shape and size?

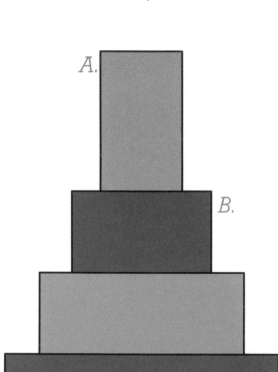

Answer: The top rectangle is the same as the second one in shape and size, but the former appears to be slimmer and longer than the latter.

Helicopter Lines

Which of the two lines that appear on top of the choppers is longer —the one of the lower helicopter or the one of the higher helicopter?

Answer: It looks as though the line of the higher helicopter is longer, but if you measure them, the line of the lower helicopter is longer.

Line Estimation

In which figure is the line divided into two equal segments: figure A or figure B?

A.

B.

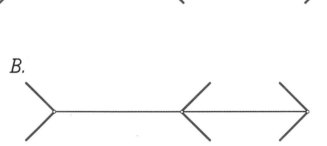

Answer: The correct answer is B. If you don't believe it, measure the segments for yourself! This optical effect is called the Müller-Lyer illusion.

Alignments

Do the two alignments of black-and-white segments converge at the top?

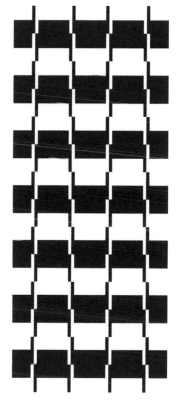

Answer: The two vertical alignments of black-and-white segments are perfectly parallel to each other.

Swollen Square

Which of these is actually a proper,
real square: A or B?

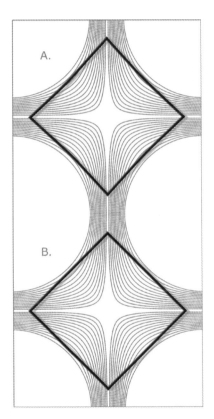

Answer: Ninety-nine percent of people say only
square B seems distorted. The reality is that square
A is distorted (concave) while square B isn't.

Astounding Dice

Are the central gray dots (pips) of the two dice the same size?

Diverging Lines?

Are the diagonal lines parallel to each other?
Is the background yellowish?

Answer: Although they appear to be divergent,
the diagonal lines are perfectly straight and parallel to
each other. The background is uniformly white.

Funny Rorschach Test
Psychological test: What does this inkblot represent for you?

Answer: Turn the page clockwise ninety degrees and you will discover a walking black bear cub and his reflection in the water.

Impossible Lego Structure
Could you build this structure with Lego blocks?

Answer: No, because it is an impossible structure. In fact, the cross-shaped top of the structure isn't congruent with the two rectangular "pillars."

Visual Test

Reproduce the outlined star. Can you trace a line within the borders of the star while you are looking in the mirror? (You may hide the drawing with a book as shown in the picture.)

Answer: No, it is in fact impossible. Tracing a drawing with the help of a mirror can be very confusing for our procedural memory.

Another Face of Paris
Find a mysterious man in this photograph.

Answer: If you look at the center of this photograph for a while, a face will suddenly emerge. Its nose is the woman's shadow.

Mysterious Animal

What animal has been carved into the wooden board?

Answer: Turn the page upside down and look at the picture from a distance. You should see a deer.

French Dilemma

Look carefully at the two sets of French baguettes in figures A and B. Are the middle-sized baguettes in each figure the same size? Or is the middle-sized baguette in A slightly longer than the one in B?

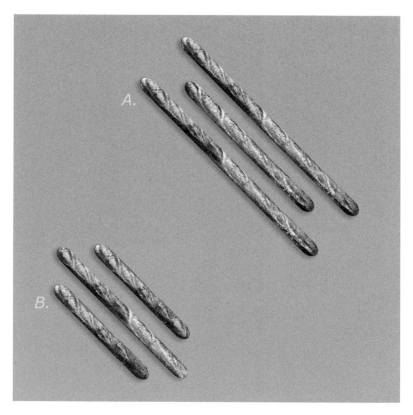

Answer: The middle-sized baguettes in A and B are both the same size. This illusion is related to the classic Müller-Lyer and Ebbinghaus illusions.

Odd Pentagon
What is wrong with this Z-shaped board?

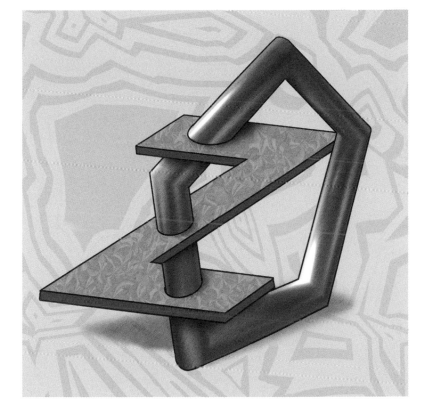

Answer: Perspectively speaking, the
Z-shaped board intersects the pentagon at
three impossible points.

Solitude
Is the old lady really alone?
How many people go with her?

Divergent Aligned Crosses?

Does each pair of columns diverge at the top?

The columns of crosses are perfectly straight and parallel to each other. This illusion is related to the Zöllner illusion.

A Baffling Structure

The crowd is attracted by a mysterious, obviously artificial artifact, coming maybe from outer space?

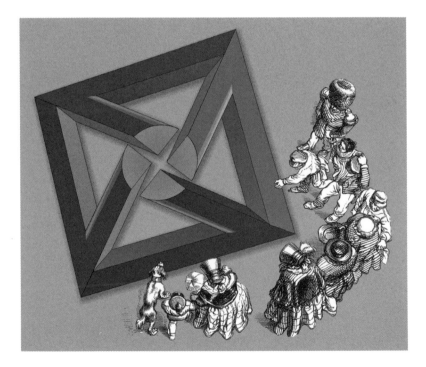

Answer: More prosaically, it's just an impossible figure!

Gray Patches

Are the gray patches that form a diamond-like pattern in the first image as bright as the clear gray patches on the right?

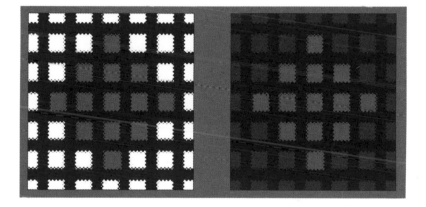

Master of Numbers

Look at this random arrangement of number photos from a distance. What do you see?

Answer: The face of the famous physicist Albert Einstein will appear.

Dark Rider

Are the rider and his faithful dog moving away
toward the horizon or toward the viewer?

Answer: It is impossible to say. This example
illustrates how difficult it is to assess the direction
of a silhouette or a shaded image.

Possible or Not?
Which one of these structures is possible to build?

Answer: None of them!

Please, Help

Can you help the boy arrange the
construction blocks into the cardboard box?

Answer: No, you cannot. The box and the play
blocks cannot exist in a real 3-D world. In fact,
if you look closely, you can clearly see that they
are impossible objects.

Plate of Fruits
Where is the painter of this still-life painting?

Answer: To see him turn the page counterclockwise ninety degrees.

Pierrot & Columbine

Find what is hidden within this picture representing Pierrot declaring his love to Columbine.

Answer: Look at the picture from a distance and you will discover a skull!

151

Origami Magic

Can you fold a piece of paper as
performed by the conjuror?

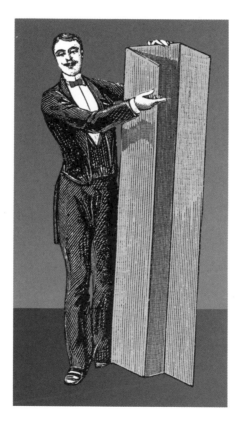

Answer: No, it is an impossible
paper-folding performance.

The Nightmare of the Mice
This terrifying black cat is on the hunt for rats.
Can you find its prey?

Answer: This is a reversible figure. The face of
the rat is blended with the nose of the cat.

Magic Smudges

Move your eyes around these groups of smudges.
Do you experience something strange?

Answer: If you move your eyes around the picture,
the smudges will appear to move slightly and float.

Mystic Apparition

Stare at the middle of the black picture for about thirty seconds. Then immediately close your eyes and tilt your head back. Keep them closed for a little while.
Do you notice something particular?

Answer: An aura surrounding a feminine face will slowly appear in your mind and then vanish. This illusion is an afterimage effect.

Changing Symbols

Look at the typographical symbols in A and B. Is each pair of letters of different size? For instance, is the "c" for copyright in the circle on your left larger than the "c" in the circle on your right?

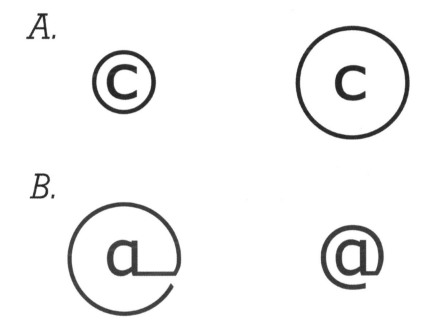

A.

B.

Globe

Which dot is the midpoint of this planisphere: the dot on the line of latitude (A) or the dot on the line of longitude (B)?

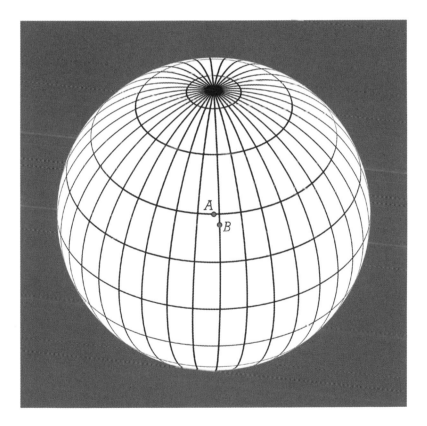

Answer: Chances are that you have answered dot B, but it is the dot A that is actually the center of the planisphere.

Staggering Wallpaper

Do you feel slightly queasy when you look at this wallpaper?
Is there something straight in the wallpaper or
is everything askew?

Answer: Although they appear to be sloped,
the columns of stacked white and black patterns
are perfectly parallel to each other. This illusion is
similar to the café wall illusion.

Curious Spirals

Which one of the circular patterns features a spiral?
Does the spiral seem to rotate or expand?

Answer: Neither of them because they are perfect concentric circles! Furthermore, these geometric figures seem to rotate slightly and expand.

Infinite Descent

Everyone knows this kind of fun spring called a Slinky that is able to go down steps one by one. Few people know that the scientist R. Penrose has built in his lab a secret staircase that allows the toy to go down infinitely without stopping. As evidence, follow with your finger the stairs and you will discover that they go down continuously. Is this the secret of perpetual motion?

Answer: No, this is just another impossible figure.

Dizzy Skyscraper

The skyscraper shown in the picture is really dizzying! Can you tell which walls are protruding and which ones are recessing? Is this a representation made with an upward or with a downward viewpoint? Is the picture right-side up, or upside down?

Shaded Squares
Are all the gray squares the same shade?

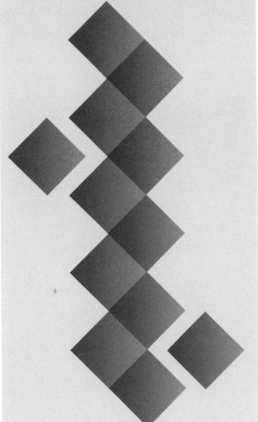

Answer: Although the second column of squares appears darker than the first one, all the gray squares are exactly the same shade. This is a neat variant of the Craik-O'Brien-Cornsweet illusion.

Play It Again
Could you play this piano bar?

Answer: If you look at the vertical space under the keys on the left and then at the surface upon which the drinks have been placed, you will see that this piano is schematically incongruent and cannot actually exist.

Domino Chaos

Are the white and black dominoes placed randomly on the tabletop? Can you crack the secret of their configuration?

Answer: This is a composite image composed of disparate smaller images that form a discrete main image. So, if you look at the picture from a distance you can see a black-and-white cat (aptly named Domino).

Contrasts

Which gray bar—A or B—corresponds to the bar lying on the contrasted background?

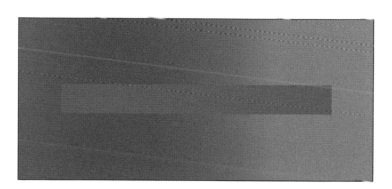

Answer: The gray bar on the contrasted background is the same shade throughout. Therefore, the answer is bar A. This illusion is based on the simultaneous brightness contrast effect.

Imaginary Circles
Do you perceive circles that appear brighter
than their surroundings?

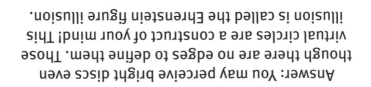

Answer: You may perceive bright discs even
though there are no edges to define them. Those
virtual circles are a construct of your mind! This
illusion is called the Ehrenstein figure illusion.

Parallel or Not?
Which pattern contains vertical alignments
of tiles that are parallel: figure A or figure B?

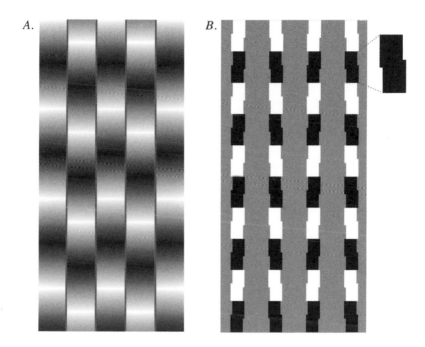

A.

B.

Answer: Both patterns contain alignments
that are parallel! Actually, an alignment consisting
of tiles with shifted gradations (figure A) or with
shifted edges (figure B) can induce a strong
visual deformation.

Tristan and Iseult

Examine the turret-like structures of the wall.
Are they convex or concave?

Answer: The turret-like structures can be interpreted as both convex and concave shapes. However, the contrasting positions of the windows indicate that the first structure is concave, and the latter, convex.

Monkey Eyes

You can see in the picture three bananas with their respective labels. Two of them are the same size. Can you guess which ones?

Answer: Bananas A and C are the same size.
This illusion is related to the Jastrow illusion, a size illusion where two curved shapes of identical measurements are placed next to each other and appear significantly different in size.

Unreal Bamboo

Do you see gray boundaries that subdivide the stem of the bamboos?

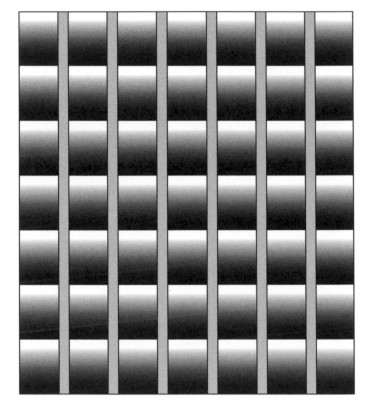

Answer: Probably yes, but those gray boundaries don't actually exist, because the hue of the bamboo is uniform. The appearance of dark gray spots is induced by the sinusoidal gratings on the background. This is a classical case of "lateral inhibition".

Magnetic Eyes

Does the woman on this book cover illustration by Aleksandr Rodchenko (1923) look directly at you, even if you move to the right or left?

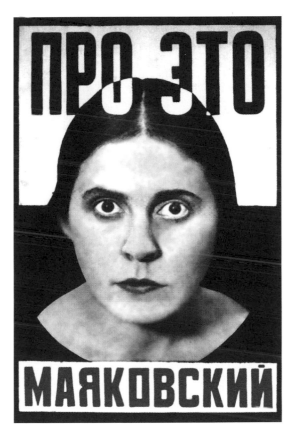

Answer: Curiously enough, from whichever point you look at the woman, she seems to be insistently gazing at you! Actually, when we see perfectly round pupils it means that they are looking at us.

Confusing Stairs
What's going on with this picture?

Answer: It is impossible to climb all the stairs in
this picture. Here, Hungarian artist István Orosz
has merged two different perspectives (and two
eras—Renaissance and modern) to create one
amazing artwork.

One Way

You have only five seconds to view the whole picture and guess what is wrong with it!

Answer: Only 20 percent of people perceive the error in the "One Way Do Not Enter" sign. In fact, most concentrate on the mirror and miss the grammatical error in the sign that says "not do enter" instead of "do not enter."

Illusive Transparencies

Balloons floating around outside a window crossed by a translucent plastic sheet or a perforated piece of paper laid on a gray rectangle?

Answer: In the picture there isn't any solid gray rectangle. Our brain interprets an image in terms of contours and light intensity. Thus, the gray section of the discs brings on the illusive appearance of a translucent gray rectangle, though the background is uniformly white!

Chaotic Evanescences

As you move your eyes around this picture, do you notice anything in particular?

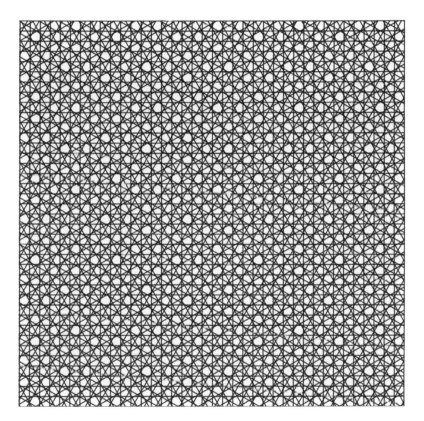

Answer: Small circles seem to appear and fade as the eye moves over them! This occurs because our visual system is searching for the best interpretation possible in this unorganized pattern.

Spinning Vortex
Are the small white dots twinkling slightly?

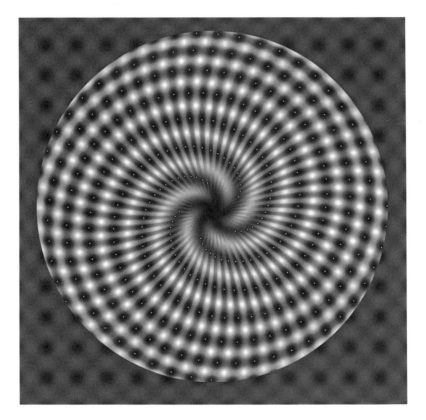

Answer: The dots on the spirals appear to vibrate and twinkle, but they are obviously still. Heavy brightness contrasts and *microsaccades* (rapid-eye random movements) induce those intermittent gleams.

Cushion Effect

Do the diamond-like shapes have wobbly corners?

Answer: Some regular patterns tend to lose their evenness when assembled in regular sets. The diamond-like shapes have right-angled corners. They also produce a fish-eye-lens effect that gives the impression of movement.

Find the Mouse
The cat is looking for the mouse. Where is it?

Upside Down

Find two big differences between the boys.
(If you can't, turn the picture upside down.)

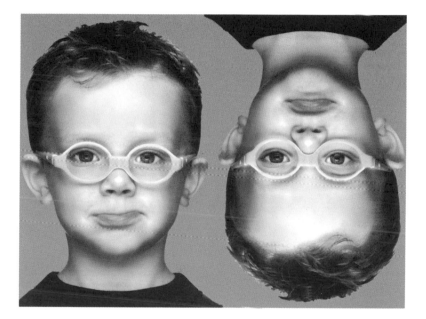

Answer: When the face of the second boy is seen right-side up, it appears quite monstrous because he has his mouth and eyes inverted. Strangely, he doesn't appear so weird when he is upside down!

Invisible Shapes
Can you see a square and a circle (or a diamond)?

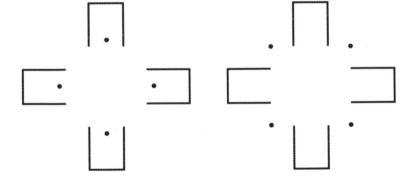

Answer: You may see a bright disc in the first
diagram and a bright square in the second one,
but these are just illusions. Their virtual contours are
formed by the interaction of dots and lines.

Heart Beats

Is the heart beating, moving, or floating
over the background?

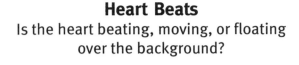

Answer: Obviously not. This is just a kinetic
optical illusion! The image is still but the contrasting
lines give a slight feeling of motion. The heart also
seems to pulsate in rhythm with the observer's
breathing.

Magic Lines

Sweep your eyes around the pattern. Do the columns of curved black & white lines diverge or converge? Did you notice anything else?

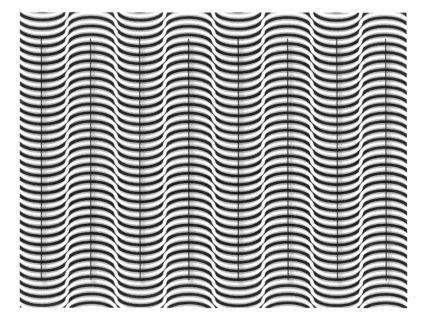

Answer: Neither. They are perfectly straight and parallel to each other. When you sweep your eyes around the pattern the vertical lines will start moving slightly. This illusion works best when seen with side vision.

Hidden Pandas

Help mother panda to find her cub and her companion!

Answer: The silhouette of the panda cub is dissimulated by the weeds on the right side of mother panda, while the face of her companion is outlined by the flowers and leaves at her left side.

Rotating?

How many spirals can you see? Do you experience something paranormal while looking at the picture?

Answer: You may see one large illusive spiral whereas there is just a series of concentric circles. Then, the spiral-like pattern seems to rotate clockwise slightly. Of course, the image is perfectly static.

Neon Illusion

Four gray stripes seem to float over the neon tubes.
Are those stripes uniformly gray?

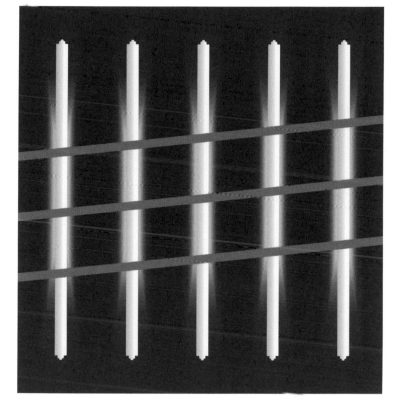

Answer: You may see intermittent dark smudges
on the stripes, but this is an illusion caused by
lateral inhibition, which enhances the contrast
of the outline of an object.

Celtic Patterns

Are the curvilinear patterns in the rectangles
A, B, C, and D the same shade?

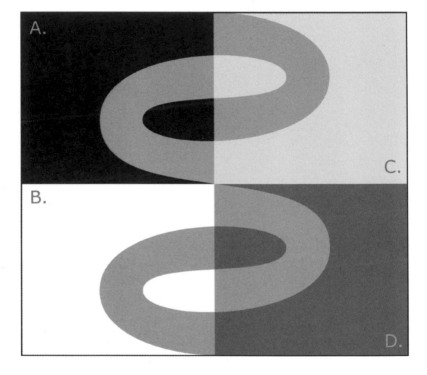

Answer: The curvilinear shapes are all of the same shade! This illusion is related to the "Benussi ring" illusion and is mainly due to the lateral inhibition of our visual system.

Polypodous Elephants
How many legs do those rolling elephants have?

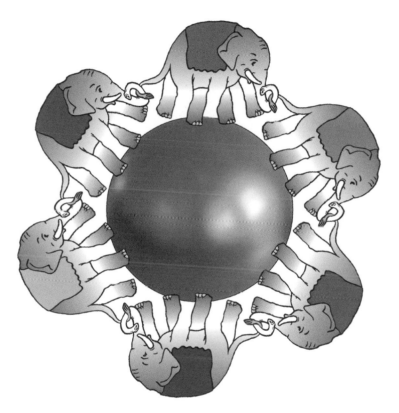

Answer: You are seeing more legs than you
should because the legs that would need to appear
have been erased and moved over to the side, filling
the legs' interspaces of the elephants.

Wandering Jellyfish

Stare at the image and imagine that the black is the deep sea. Concentrate and cast your eyes around the groups of jellyfish. Do they start to move in opposite directions?

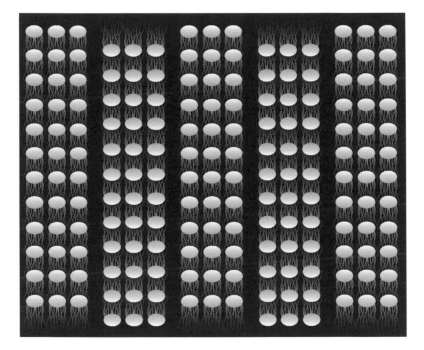

Answer: This illusory motion is related to the central drift illusion. The factor that induces this illusion may be the difference in contrast between the inner and outer areas of the "moving" objects.

PART 3:
Try These Puzzles and Find
Your Answers in the Back

Amazing Tribar
Is the triangular sculpture in the background possible?

Answer on Page 258

T-wist

Do the capital letters of the word TILT seem to "dance" or are they perfectly aligned?

Answer on Page 258

Las Meninas
Where is the main subject in this painting by
the Spanish artist Diego Velázquez?

Answer on Page 259

Somnolent Length

Which one of these beds is as long as it's wide?

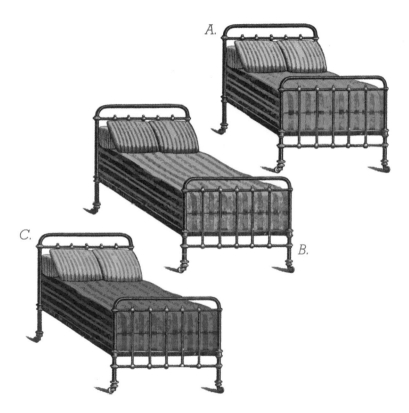

Answer on Page 259

Mind Reading

Here is an interesting mind-reading experiment.
Follow these steps:

Step 1) Take a look at all the crosses in
the picture, raise your arm, and repeat
"crickroc" twice.

Step 2) Hold your breath. Count to three and
place a forefinger on one of the crosses.
Hold it firmly there for seven seconds.

Step 3) Breathe, take your finger off the cross,
and count to three.

Answer on Page 260

The Impossible Swiss Cross

Copy and cut out the four geometric shapes.
Can you assemble them to form a Swiss cross?

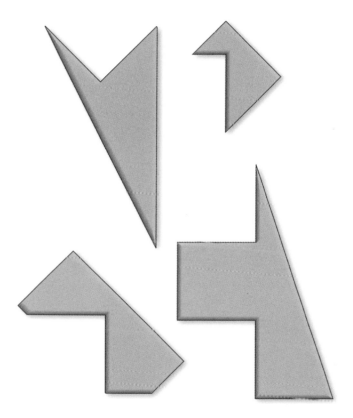

Answer on Page 260

Pastry Puzzle

Alter the fresh 8-shaped pastry in order to thread the stick into its second loop. You cannot unthread the stick from the pastry or cut the pastry in any way.

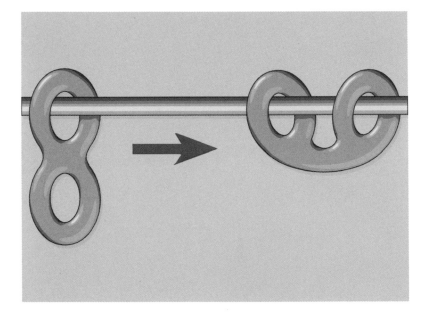

Answer on Page 261

Elephant or Bull?

The bull and the elephant, representing respectively Lord Shiva and Ganesh, are a recurrent motif in Hindu mythology as shown in this ceiling painting of the Sri Meenakshi temple in Madurai. Does the head portrayed belong to an elephant or a bull? Or could it be both at the same time?

Answer on Page 261

How Many Angels?
How many angels are represented in the picture?

Answer on Page 262

Find the Hidden Shape

Follow your own star (like the one in fig. A) and find it in the pattern below.

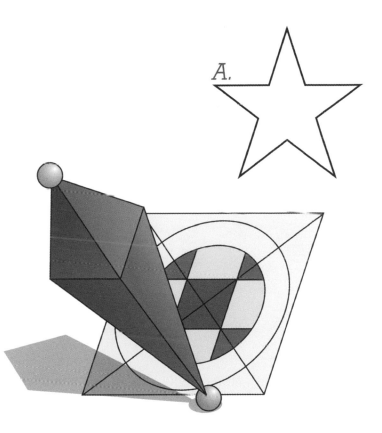

A.

Answer on Page 262

Pointing Fingers

In your opinion, which forefinger points exactly to the middle of the shape's height: A or B? Please, explain what influenced your choice!

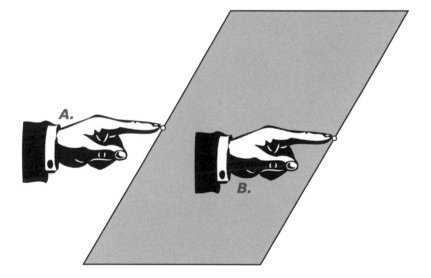

Answer on Page 262

Perfect Square

In which figure, A or B, will you obtain a perfect square by connecting the small white dots?

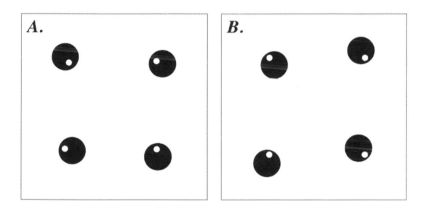

Answer on Page 263

A Little Giant
Is the boy a giant?

Answer on Page 263

At Right Angle?

One of the angles of the tubular cross is ninety degrees.
Help Jean Vidocq, the Sun King's architect, find it!

Answer on Page 263

Pisa Tower Paintings
Which of these paintings hangs slightly askew?

Answer on Page 264

Nightmare Prisons
Something in this Gothic picture by Italian artist
Piranesi is wrong. Can you tell what?

Answer on Page 264

Visual Estimation

Estimate the circumference of the rim of each cylinder. Try to guess which cylinder has a circumference as long as its height.

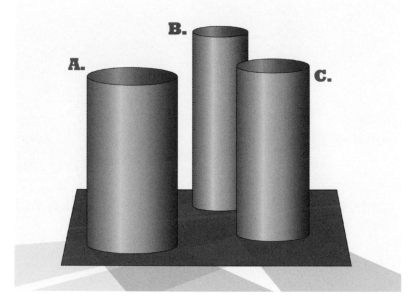

Answer on Page 265

The Magic Easter Egg

Reproduce and cut out the three-piece puzzle shown in the picture. Rearrange the pieces in order to make the egg disappear.

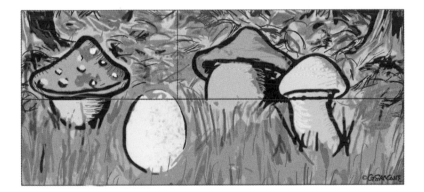

Answer on Page 265

A Matter of Clarity

In which case (A or B) are the vertical gray slices not the same shade as the horizontal slices?

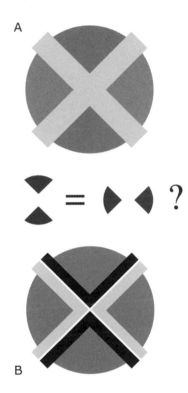

Answer on Page 266

Black & White Camouflage
What does this black-and-white picture represent?

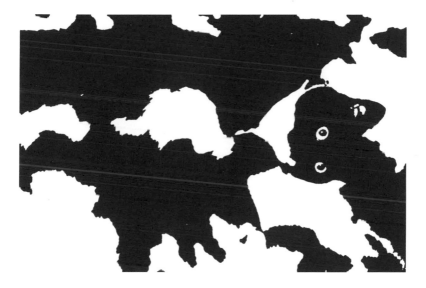

Answer on Page 266

Hidden Polygons

Find the cross (a) and the eight-pointed star (b) in the square.

a.   *b.*

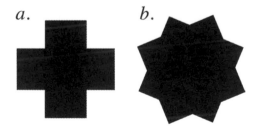

Answer on Page 267

Mental Block

Figure A represents a broken capital "T." Reproduce the puzzle pieces and try to fix the letter (as shown in figure C) by placing figure B into the puzzle. Even though the piece doesn't seem to fit the puzzle, don't be skeptical. Use your visual thinking to achieve this challenge!

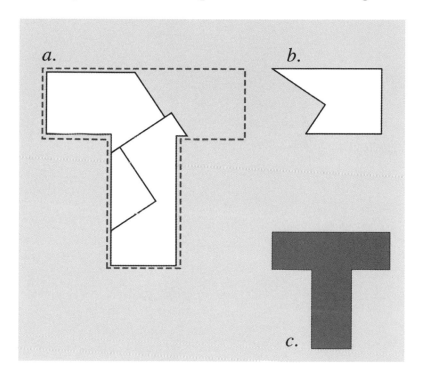

a.

b.

c.

Answer on Page 267

Bunch of Babies
How many babies?

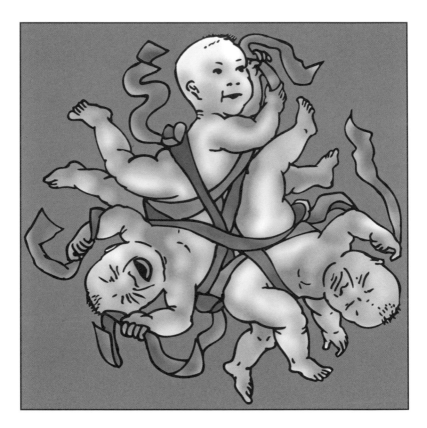

Answer on Page 267

Good Vibes

Are some portions of this vibrating pattern clearer than other ones? Can you perceive two sets of distinct rectangles?

Answer on Page 268

Dovetail

The assembly shown in the picture looks like an impossible construction. However, try to imagine how the two triangle-shaped pieces were assembled.

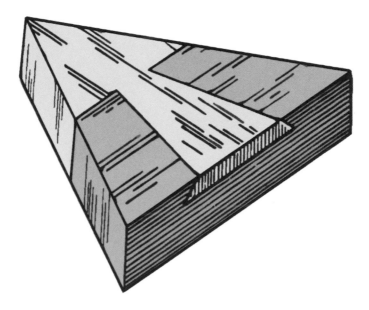

Answer on Page 268

Find the Hidden Shape

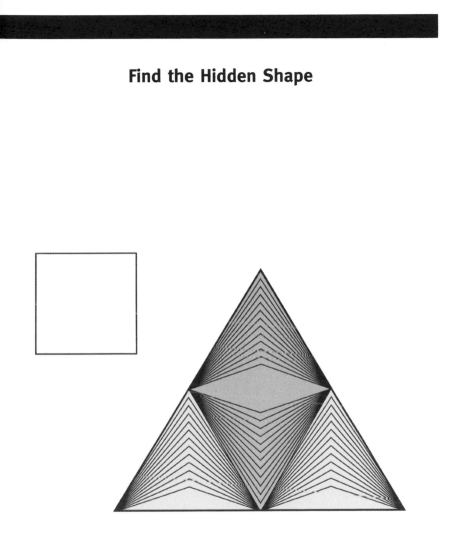

Answer on Page 268

Find the Prism

The outlines of the prism are hidden in the pattern on the right.

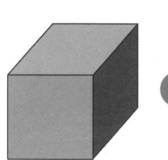

Answer on Page 269

William Tell Illusion

How many arrows do you see? Are you sure?
Count them again.

Answer on Page 269

Give the Boxer a Ring!
It is easy to draw two squares using all eight dots, but can you make just one perfect square (the ring) by connecting ALL the dots?

Answer on Page 270

Priming Completion

Answer on Page 270

Where You Bean?
Try to find the child in the coffee beans!

Answer on Page 271

More Arrows

Answer on Page 271

Puzzling Planks

Which way are the planks facing? If you see errors in the orientation of the items can you redraw them correctly?

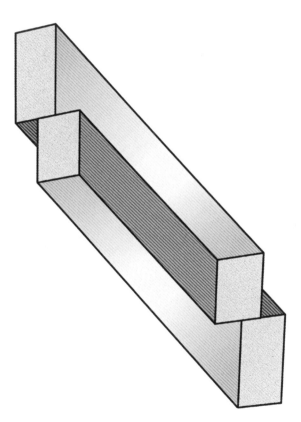

Answer on Page 272

Woman Ubiquity

Is this woman looking toward you or away from you?

Answer on Page 272

Magic Queen

A card representing a mysterious queen of spades is cut into five pieces. But when we turn these pieces over and try to reassemble the card facedown, one piece is left over. How is it possible?

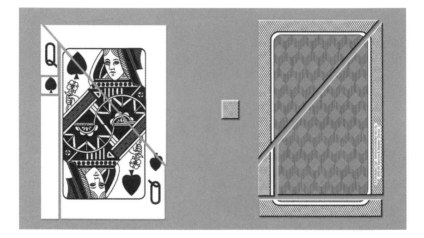

Answer on Page 273

Evanescent Bird

Reproduce and cut out the three puzzle pieces. Then, rearrange the pieces to make an additional bird appear!

Answer on Page 273

Disentanglement

Is it possible to free the scissors without cutting the string? As you can see, a hooked nail holds the string to a desk.

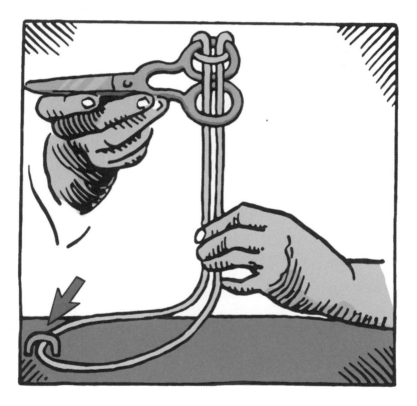

Answer on Page 274

Gradient Camouflage

How many distinct balls can you perceive
in the sand ripples?

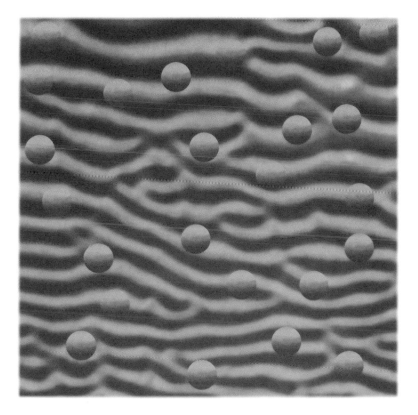

Answer on Page 275

Horse and Rider

Compare the whole width of the horse (A), from tail to head, to its height (B). Is the horse taller or wider?

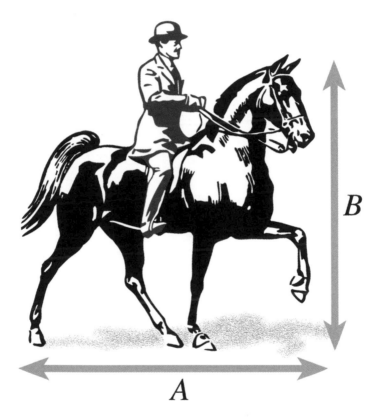

Answer on Page 275

The Time of Cherries

There are two hidden birds somewhere inside the photograph. How long will it take you to spot them?

Answer on Page 276

Giraffe vs. Dog

Is the giraffe taller than the length of the dog, or is the dog longer than the height of the giraffe?

Answer on Page 276

Misleading Directions

Are you good at visually orienting yourself? Are you sure? Then take this test: A pointed finger is printed on both sides of an octagonal racket. Try now to guess which direction the finger points to in B and C!

Front   Back

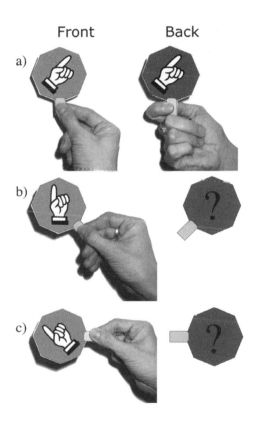

a)

b)

c)

Answer on Page 277

Immanent Presence

A famous physicist is hidden within this scene.
Can you guess who and where he is?

Answer on Page 277

Visual Estimation
Is the area of the outer dark ring larger or smaller than the inner clear ring?

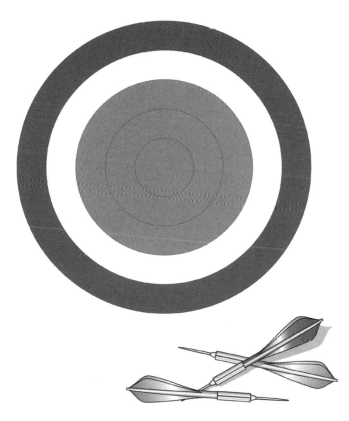

Answer on Page 278

Invisible Squares

Try to find as many squares as you can in
this geometric diagram.

Answer on Page 278

The Dream of the Beast

Look at Frankenstein's monster from approximately seven to eight feet (two to four meters) away, and you will see what he is dreaming about.

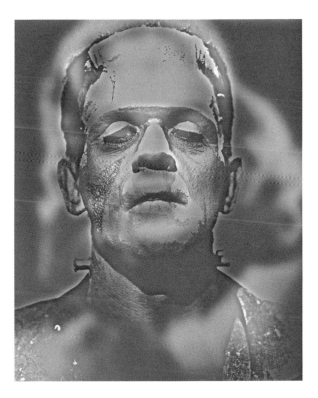

Answer on Page 279

R's Dilemma

Observe the surfaces of the three R's.
There are at least two R-shapes that are congruent
(equal). Can you find them?

Answer on Page 279

Visual Riddle

When Fred the hamster starts running, will the hand of the speedometer of the exercise device turn clockwise or counterclockwise?

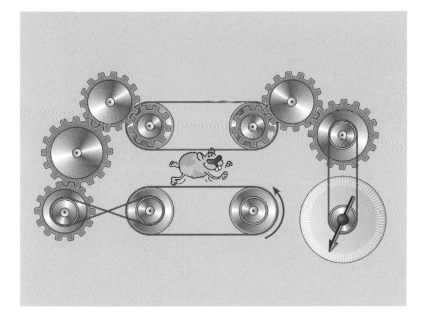

Answer on Page 279

Un-decidable Box

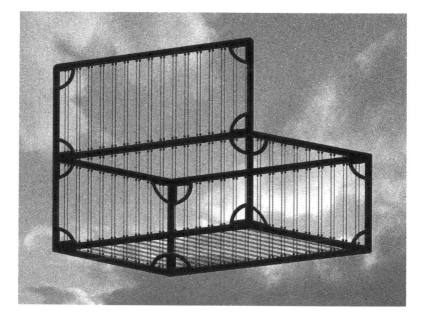

Answer on Page 280

Borromini's False Perspective

The Palazzo Spada in Rome, Italy, has a strange alcove where people seem to grow as they walk away down the corridor! This effect is due to an ingenious trick of the Renaissance architect Francesco Borromini. He made the corridor, which is only about thirty-three feet (ten meters) long, look far longer—like three-times longer. How did he do it?

Answer on Page 280

Coin Estimation

Which of the five coins exactly covers the width of the gray-and-black checkerboard A? Which coin has a diameter that matches the height of the stack of coins B?

A.

B.

Answer on Page 281

Oriental Fan
Do the pleated surfaces of the fan have the same shade?

Answer on Page 281

Impossible Furniture

In this waiting room there are two impossible objects hidden among the retro furniture. Try to find them! Are you able to perceive one of the plastic armchairs from two different perspectives?

Answer on Page 282

Hidden Zebras
Find the other three zebras within this picture.

Answer on Page 282

Visuospatial Test

Is it possible to reproduce this pyramid-like figure just by cutting three times and folding a single piece of paper? (You cannot cut the paper into two or more different pieces.)

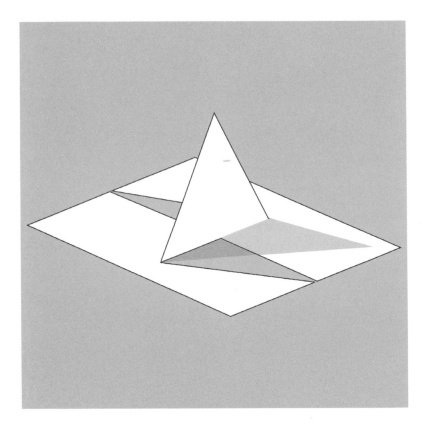

Answer on Page 283

Halloween Popcorns
How many spooky skulls can you
spot in this bowl of popcorn?

Answer on Page 283

Tangram Visual Paradox

Reproduce and cut out the seven tangram pieces. Try to form the white figures (A), and then their black counterparts with a missing triangle (B). In both cases, you have to use ALL seven pieces. Is this possible?

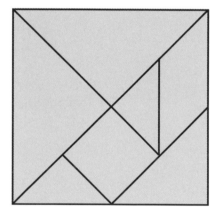

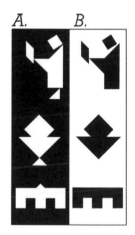

A.   B.

Answer on Page 284

Puzzling Mirrors

Observe both katoptrons (sort of antique Greek mirrors) A and B. Katoptron B is the mirror image of katoptron A, yet something is wrong. Can you spot the difference between the two objects?

Answer on Page 284

Ambiguous Message

Can you believe that this nice girl sports a T-shirt with a hate message? No. Surely there's a hidden message somewhere in the picture. Can you find it?

Answer on Page 285

Book Ends
Which line, A or B, is connected to point C?

Answer on Page 285

Clean Carpets

At the Palace Hotel, two cleaners have to vacuum the carpets in the corridors on the first floor. In your opinion, which has less work to do: the one with carpet A or the one with carpet B?

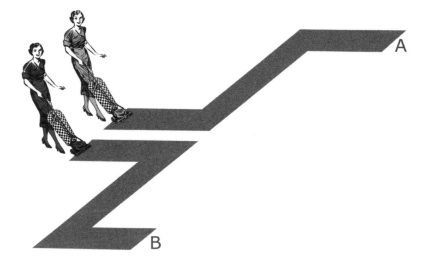

Answer on Page 285

Visual Labyrinths

Observe the three spiral labyrinths A, B, and C. Although they might look the same, they present some fundamental differences! In fact, which ant entering and wandering through its respective maze will finally reach the desired sugar cubes?

Answer on Page 286

The Ambassadors Holbein

Answer on Page 286

Hidden Right Angles

How many ninety-degree angles are hidden
in this 3-D rendering?

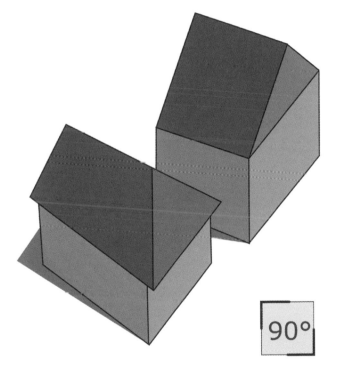

90°

Answer on Page 287

Balls Against Newton's Principles

Kokichi Sugihara, a mathematical engineer at Meiji University in Japan, built a simple set of four ramps, arranged in a cross, on which colored balls seem to magically roll uphill, as if pulled by a magnet toward the center of the structure. Can you guess how the trick works?

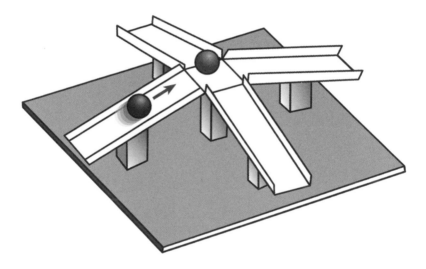

Answer on Page 287

Impossible Roof Defies Gravity

Here is the latest seemingly impossible construction of Kokichi Sugihara: a gravity-defying roof that appears to attract and balance balls on its edge! Can you guess the visual trick that underlies this illusion?

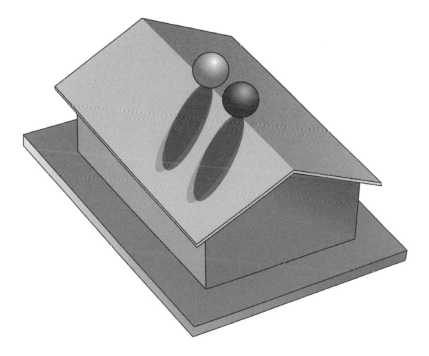

Answer on Page 288

Star Contrast

Are the octagons A and B within the yin-yang symbol the same hue and brightness?

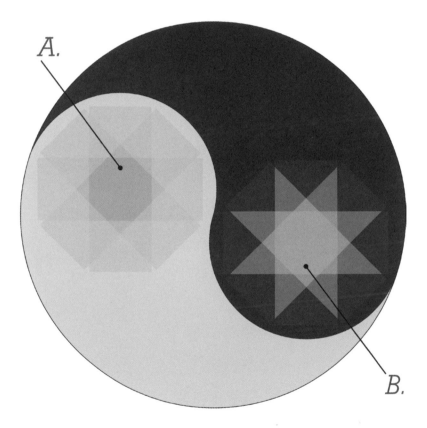

A.

B.

Answer on Page 288

ANSWERS

Amazing Tribar - Page 190

The sculpture represents an "Impossible Triangle" (tribar). To achieve such a visual effect, the photograph has to be taken from a precise point of view. In the illustration you can see two different points of view of the same sculpture.

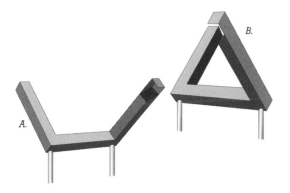

T-wist - Page 191

Answer: The letters seem slanted in spite of the fact that each of them is perfectly aligned and straight!

Las Meninas - Page 192
Answer: No, it is not the cute little girl. The main subject is actually outside the painting! You can see the artist at work portraying the royal couple King Philip IV of Spain and Queen Mariana of Austria— who are the real subject of the painting. The mirror in the background reflects the king and queen smiling at their daughter and courtiers as they pose.

Somnolent Length - Page 193
Answer: Chances are you have answered bed C, but the correct answer is bed B. Estimating the dimension of objects on paper is quite different than in real three-dimensional life!

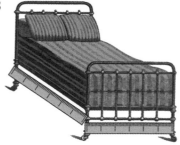

Mind Reading - Page 194
Answer: Strangely enough, most people will always choose the circled cross shown in the figure below!

The Impossible Swiss Cross - Page 195
Answer: The outline of the cross is defined by blank and solid spaces.

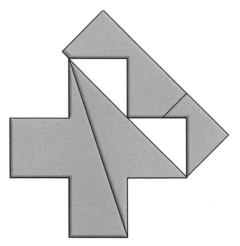

Pastry Puzzle - Page 196
Answer: You can solve this puzzle using a topological method called continuous transformation. Topology deals with the ways that surfaces can be twisted, bent, pulled, or otherwise deformed from one shape to another without tearing or cutting.

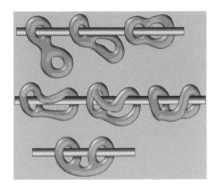

Elephant or Bull? - Page 197
Answer: The iconic representation of a bull and an elephant fighting and blending their heads together symbolizes the duality of opposites that become one. This kind of image induces a phenomenon of multistable perception in the viewer. There are many variants of the illusion in different temples all over India.

Rameshwaram temple, Rameshwaram

Dharasuram temple, Tamil Nadu

Birla Mandir temple, Shahad

Jalakanteshwara temple, Vellore

How Many Angels? - Page 198
Answer: See illustrations A and B.
Two different pairs of angels!

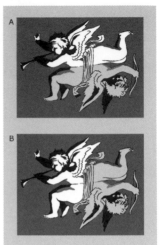

Find the Hidden Shape - Page 199
Answer:

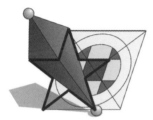

Pointing Fingers - Page 200
Answer: Strangely enough, most are convinced that both fingers point at the same level (although the one on the right appears to be lower). Actually, only finger B points to the middle of the shape's height.

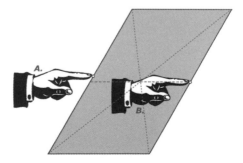

Perfect Square - Page 201
Answer: In figure B!

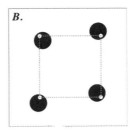

A Little Giant - Page 202
Answer: The boy appears to be a giant because of the particular trapezoidal configuration of the room. The actual position of the woman is farther away than it appears. Such a special room that distorts sizes is called an Ames room.

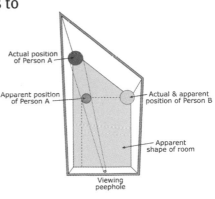

At Right Angle? - Page 203
Answer: See illustration to the right. Because of the apparent perspective bias, the ninety-degree angle does not look very convincing.

Pisa Tower Paintings - Page 204
Answer:

Nightmare Prisons - Page 205

Answer: In terms of perspective, the arch—which is in the background, emphasized with a bold dark outline—is incorrectly aligned with the lower part of the architectural structure, in the foreground, also emphasized with a bold dark outline.

Visual Estimation - Page 206

Answer: We tend to underestimate circular objects. You have probably answered cylinder A or C. The circumference of a circle is calculated by multiplying the diameter by pi, that is, by 3.14. So, the cylinder having a height and a rim of the same length is cylinder B (whose height is three-times and a bit greater than its diameter).

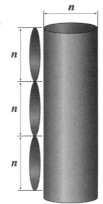

The Magic Easter Egg - Page 207

Answer: When you transpose the two upper rectangular pieces, you will still have three mushrooms but the egg will have disappeared. The principle of this visual conjuring trick is that the egg did not actually disappear—it has just been redistributed among the other pictorial subjects.

A Matter of Clarity - Page 208
Answer: See figures A and B to the right.
In A, the vertical slices are different from
the horizontal slices.

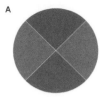

A

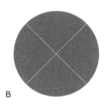

B

Black & White Camouflage - Page 209
Answer: A black-and-white spotted cat lying on a black-
and-white cow-skin rug. Figure and ground have been
deliberately obscured to challenge and illustrate the
importance of prior experience to discern the meaning of
an image.

Hidden Polygons - Page 210
Answer:

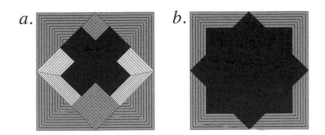

Mental Block - Page 211
Answer:

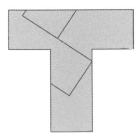

Bunch of Babies - Page 212
Answer: There are seven distinct babies (three baby heads with interchangeable bodies).

Good Vibes - Page 213
Answer: The lines are evenly black, though some portions of the pattern may appear gray or even navy. There are actually two distinct sets of rectangles as shown in the figures A and B.

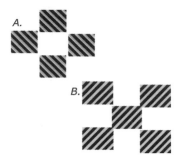

Dovetail - Page 214
Answer:

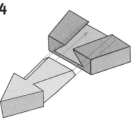

Find the Hidden Shape - Page 215
Answer:

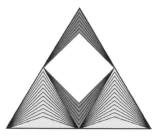

Find the Prism - Page 216
Answer:

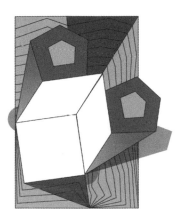

William Tell Illusion - Page 217
Answer: In this figure-ground illusion it is possible to perceive eight arrows.

Give the Boxer a Ring! - Page 218
Answer:

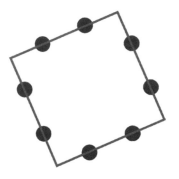

Priming Completion - Page 219
Answer: Mental expectations always affect perception and influence how we understand our world.

Where You Bean? - Page 220
Answer: To the right

More Arrows - Page 221
Answer: There are forty-eight arrows in all! There are two sets of arrows that are not easy to perceive. See A and B below. This is a figure-ground perceptual illusion based on the fact that we tend to perceive a figure that stands out from the background.

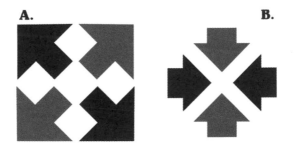

Puzzling Planks - Page 222
Answer: This is an impossible figure, as the side of one plank becomes the side of another.

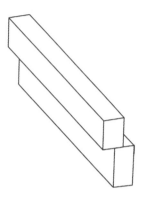

Woman Ubiquity - Page 223
Answer: Actually, you can see her from behind or, if you hide the shaded arm with a pencil as shown, you will see her face on. This is to demonstrate that the same picture can take on new meaning according to the context within which it is perceived.

Magic Queen - Page 224
Answer: Because the imprinting of one side does not correspond to the other side. As you can see below, only one piece has a coherent imprinting on both sides. The card facedown (when a piece is left) is simply different and slightly smaller than the card face-up.

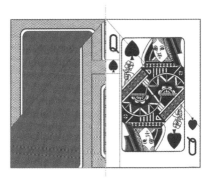

Evanescent Bird - Page 225
Answer: The bird in the puzzle (re)appears or disappears because of the redistribution of single image portions. The more birds there are, the thinner they are.

Disentanglement - Page 226
Answer: See figure below. Loosen the loop knot (figure a) and pull it through the opposite finger hole (figure b). Then, pass it all the way over the scissors (figure c). Finally, pull on the other end of the loop string to free the scissors.

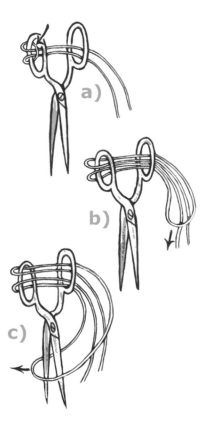

Gradient Camouflage - Page 227
Answer: There are exactly twenty-four balls. Observe how the same arrangement of dots filled with a gradient hue seems different when lying on sand ripples. Some dots become more apparent, while others become quite invisible—though all the dots in the picture have exactly the same gradient and hue. Gradient-gradient illusions are very common in nature. Most animals display a gradient camouflage to blend in with the surrounding environment.

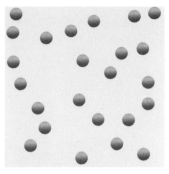

Horse and Rider - Page 228
Answer: Most people think it's wider; however, the picture of the horse fits in a perfect square. So, it is as high as it is wide.

The Time of Cherries - Page 229
Answer: See figure below.

Giraffe vs. Dog - Page 230
Answer: Of course, the height of the giraffe equals the whole length of the dog. The majority of people answer that the dog is longer.

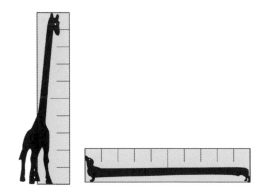

Misleading Directions - Page 231
Answer: See figures to the right.
Eighty percent of people fail
this test. To understand why
the fingers point to an apparent
unexpected direction, you have
to consider that the rackets in B
and C use two symmetry axes
instead of one: the vertical axis
of the person who holds the
racket and the axis of the handle
of the racket.

b)

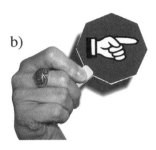

c)

Immanent Presence - Page 232
Answer: See picture to the right.
The face of Albert Einstein is
embedded in this figure-ground
illusion. Just look at the picture
from a distance and
his face will appear in the
background.

Visual Estimation - Page 233
Answer: See figure below. The area of the outer dark ring is the same as the inner clear ring.

The area of the outer ring is:
$5^2\pi - 4^2\pi = \pi(5^2 - 4^2) = 9\pi = $ **28.27...** square units

The area of the clear disc is:
$3^2\pi = 9\pi = $ **28.27...** square units

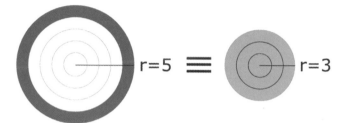

Invisible Squares - Page 234
Answer: See figure to the right. There are thirteen squares in the picture!

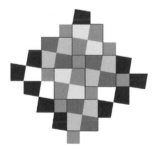

The Dream of the Beast - Page 235

Answer: When you see the picture close-up, the fine details of the monster dominate, but when you observe it from a distance, the larger, more blurred tones become more coherent and, in this case, a beautiful Marilyn Monroe.
As shown opposite.

R's Dilemma - Page 236

Answer: Incredibly, the white R and the black R coincide exactly when superimposed!

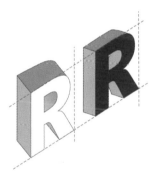

Visual Riddle - Page 237

Answer: Counterclockwise.

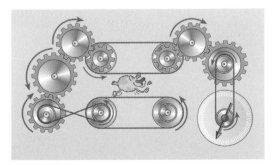

Un-decidable Box - Page 238

Answer: See figure to the right. This wrought-iron trunk occupies two different spatial positions.

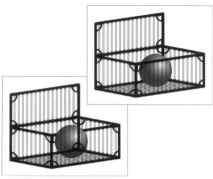

Borromini's False Perspective - Page 239

Answer: Borromini made the corridor look far longer by making both sides converge and by having the floor lean slightly upward, reducing the height of the columns as they gradually recede from the entrance. You can see this in the sketches representing the bird's-eye view in figure A and the lateral view in figure B.

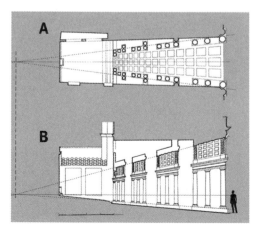

Coin Estimation - Page 240

Answer: The one cent! This illustrates the difficulty in estimating the real size of circular objects.

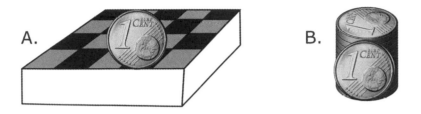

A.

B.

Oriental Fan - Page 241

Answer: Yes. The thin dark and bright shades that surround the surfaces give the overall visual impression that they are of two different alternating tones.

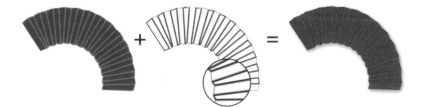

Impossible Furniture - Page 242
Answer:

Hidden Zebras - Page 243
Answer:

Visuospatial Test - Page 244
Answer:

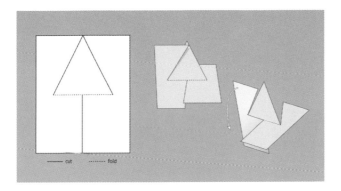

Halloween Popcorns - Page 245
Answer:

Tangram Visual Paradox - Page 246
Answer: Yes, it is possible because, in reality, the related figures are slightly different in size. In the counterparts, the missing piece is compensated for by a larger silhouette.

Puzzling Mirrors - Page 247
Answer: The objects A and B both contain a decorative spiral-like design. However, the design in object A is actually two distinct spirals, while the design in object B represents just one double spiral.

A. 2 spirals

B. 1 double spiral

Ambiguous Message - Page 248

Answer: The hidden message is "love." To transform "hate" into "love," place the image in front of a mirror.

Book Ends - Page 249

Answer: Line A.

Clean Carpets - Page 250

Answer: Both carpets are the same length.

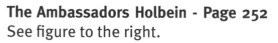

Visual Labyrinths - Page 251
Answer: Labyrinth B shows a continuous double-spiral path that leads to the sugar cubes.

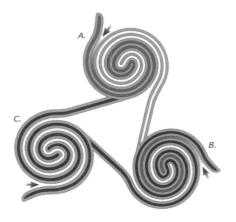

The Ambassadors Holbein - Page 252
See figure to the right.

Hidden Right Angles - Page 253

Answer: Eight! Most people locate up to six relatively easily. A tough one to find is that on the upper side of the house in the background. Some angles may not look like right angles, but this is due to a trick of the apparent perspective.

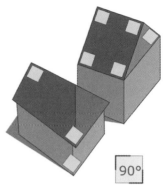

Balls Against Newton's Principles - Page 254

Answer: It's all a question of vantage point! In this trick of perspective, the slopes actually tilt downward. In fact, what is happening is that the orientations of the slopes are perceived oppositely, and hence the descending motion is misinterpreted as ascending motion.
You can enjoy the video of this funny illusion here:
http://illusioncontest.neuralcorrelate.com/2010/impossible-motion-magnet-like-slopes/

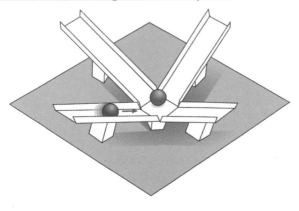

Impossible Roof Defies Gravity - Page 255

Answer: See illustration to the right. When the house is rotated, its true form is revealed! The drawing shows the structure seen from behind. According to Sugihara, our brain seems to choose the most rectangular configuration when it tries to make sense of features that can have different interpretations.

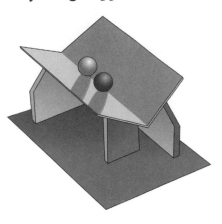

Star Contrast - Page 256

Answer: Yes, they are. The simultaneous brightness contrast makes them look very different!